UPCOUNTRY ODYSSEY

CYCLING SOLO AT 68 FROM FLORIDA TO CANADA THROUGH THE APPALACHIAN MOUNTAINS

BY

FRANK A. BOSTWICK

UPCOUNTRY ODYSSEY

CYCLING SOLO AT 68 FROM FLORIDA TO CANADA THROUGH THE APPALACHIAN MOUNTAINS

BY

FRANK A. BOSTWICK

First Edition
First Printing
© Copyright 1998, Frank Bostwick

ISBN: 1-891118-29-3

Published by
Wind Canyon Publishing, Inc.
P.O. Box 1445
Niceville, Florida 32588-1445

Editor: George Jaquith
Layout/Design: Becky Jaquith
Cover Design: Wind Canyon Publishing, Inc. ©1998

Wind Canyon Publishing, Inc. offers other book titles. Wind Canyon, Inc. offers software applications work related to book publishing, including converting titles to multimedia CD-ROM discs and other computer formats. For further information, including details regarding the submission of manuscripts, contact the above address.

ACKNOWLEDGMENTS

Many lovers of words and ideas helped me with this narrative. Special thanks to Rowena Bartmon who edited the initial chapters with fine precision; Tim Grinder, whose sense of style and pace were extraordinary, and Ann Mock, whose flair for editing is professional in every way. Also of generous help was Carolyn Cerney, who separated bushels of chaff from essential grains of editorial wheat as the tale began to grow. Others whose advice was really appreciated were Steve Brahlek, Clare, Dick and Gale Reed, George Bartmon, Francine Mohr, Bob Mohr, Dr. Ted Menter, Jeff Ferber, Nancy Lamb, Phoebe Cartwright, Louise Hall, Dianna Collier, Linda Leeds, Joseph McColly, Roosevelt and Eva Blair, Tom Kaufman, Gladys Hanna, Cindy Bostwick, Melissa Bostwick Saddler, Mark Bostwick, B.C. Brewer, Tom Kaufman, Roberta Stevenson, Hank Martin, Leroy Reed, Greg Siple, Mary Ellen and Wilbur Shelton.

INTRODUCTION

Come along with me on my mini-odyssey during the autumn of my life. In my 69th year, I became a self-contained, touring cyclist for 32 days. I pedaled alone from South Florida to Canada, averaging 54 miles a day, upcountry through nine states. My excellent adventure began with a kind of "shakedown cruise" around Lake Okeechobee, west of West Palm Beach. Then, I headed north through the Appalachian mountains to the Midwest and beyond.

You may find a few chuckles, a couple of sighs, and perhaps discover an insight or two about your own life from my bicycle touring experience. Following my bliss worked for me. You try, too. That's what self-containment is all about.

I rode *Sir Walter*, my 20-year old, steel-framed Raleigh Super Cruiser bicycle. We traveled 1668 miles. I pitched my pup tent beside back-roads two of every three nights. It's the essence of Outside.

When some of my contemporaries heard I was going to ride a bike alone from South Florida to Canada, their comments varied: "Are you nuts; at your age?" "What about all those crazies out there?" Or, "Why risk being a victim?" Also, "Aren't these flat Florida roads challenge enough?"

I'd try to explain my desire for self-containment. Don't most of us go through our lives relying on others to help steer us safely along the path? If we're lucky, our parents get us started. Then, our teachers take over. Most of us also have plenty of advice from family and friends about choosing life's partners. Many times, our choice of occupation is strongly influenced by others. As I did, we typically move from home to school to job and to marriage with mentors at our elbows, suggesting, nudging us.

Untold millions of people follow a similar path through life. However, as retirement approached, I realized I had not really stepped back to examine my life. It seemed to have passed through its spring, summer and early fall at full tilt, feeding on its own momentum.

How often I had heard a half-joking refrain from those already retired. "For better or for worse, sure, but not for lunch." They were not necessarily critical of the constant proximity of their spouses. It was just that in their pre-retirement days, their lives were propelled by forces put into motion 30 or 40 years before. Now, out of the workaday mainstream, they were faced by decisions of what to do with all that free time. I, too, had to choose.

I began to realize how seldom I had relied entirely upon my own decisions. I wondered if, over a significantly extended period of time, I could enjoy being truly alone, outside, paring my decisions down to the minimal questions of food, clothing and shelter while literally going somewhere, on a quest, a private adventure separate from home, loved ones, and professional pursuits. Could I endure my own company for, say, a month?

I always had loved books about adventures, both large and small, physical or intellectual. Especially appealing for me in later years were the works of Henry David Thoreau. A particular phrase of his kept nagging. He had spelled out so well in Walden what was beginning to noodle around inside me, insisting upon examination. I, too, for just a short time, wanted "to live deliberately, to front only the essential facts of life, and see if I could learn what it had to teach, and not, when I came to die, discover that I had not lived."

Oh, I wasn't anxious to head for Walden Pond to build my own cabin and live in it for 24 months, the way he did more than 100 years ago. But the open road did beckon, perhaps for the same reason he gave for his Walden adventure — so that I could "live deliberately." Thoreau had his cabin. I had my bicycle.

Happily, my children had grown successfully into their own decision-making years, and my wonderfully supportive wife understood my unquenched thirst for outdoor adventures not necessarily confined to say, man-made contours of fairways, bunkers, sand traps, and greens.

How does one prepare for an overland cycling tour? By getting comfortable with that Outside, both on and off the saddle. I began by joining the West Palm Beach Bicycle Club. I cycled alone and with others for three years, primarily on weekends. We would average between 20 and 30 miles per ride. I became acclimated to cycling in traffic, respecting stop signs, stop lights and motorists. Tractor-trailer trucks were especially formidable, and smart cyclists have a healthy respect for them, but bicycles also are legally allowed on those roads.

As all sensible road cyclists do, I staked out that three to six inches on either side of the white line on the right-hand edge of the highway, flowing with the traffic, hoping for smooth shoulders, settling for a foot of whatever available space there was on the far right.

Camping came easily. I had spent the first 16 summers of my youth in central Wisconsin. My "room" alongside our family cottage on Gilbert Lake was a 9x12-foot canvas tent. Boy Scouting reinforced my outdoor skills.

Now that time had come when I was able to succumb to what Thoreau labeled "a subtle magnetism in Nature, which, if we unconsciously yield to it, will direct us aright." That magnetism can truly be felt on a touring bike in the springtime. Join me and *Sir Walter* — self-contained.

CONTENTS

CHAPTER	TITLE	PAGE

Introduction

1 Okeechobee Shakedown Cruise — 1
   Cycling around Florida's "Big Lake"

2 North Along the Atlantic — 13
   The first leg to Canada

3 Perch Bones and Places to Perch — 25
   Fine-tuning saddles and sites

4 Wind, Sand and Time — 33
   Northerly breezes slow pace

5 Detours, Birdsong and Swimming Holes — 43
   How to turn trouble into triumph

6 Drive-by Shooters, Famous Poet, and Fans — 53
   Southern hospitality adds spice to touring

7 On the Road to Damascus — 73
   Steep mountains and a serious concern

8 "The Friendliest Town on the Trail" — 85
   Why hikers, bikers and tourists visit Damascus

9 Dogs, Deer and the Courage of Turtles — 93
   Some quadrupeds fight, most flee

10 Cars, Trucks and Other Highway Hazards — 105
   Safety tips and "kissing bridges"

11 Riding Through My Heartland — 119
   Level riding changes pace

12 Bodiless Silk and Big City Blight — 129
   Wind on grass, then urban turmoil

13 Fishing in Time's Stream — 141
   Don't let age myths mar your bliss.

Appendix A — 147

Appendix B — 148

To my wife, Kathryn.
Her love, trust and faith in me provided
the freedom to follow roads less traveled by.

Upcountry Odyssey

Cycling Solo at 68
from
Florida to Canada
through
The Appalachian Mountains

"People say that what we're all seeking is a meaning for life. I don't think that's what we're really seeking. I think that what we're seeking is an experience of being alive, so that our life experiences on a purely physical plane will have resonances within our own innermost being and reality, so that we actually feel the rapture of being alive."

— Joseph Campbell
The Power of Myth

CHAPTER ONE

OKEECHOBEE SHAKEDOWN CRUISE

An absolutely new prospect is a great happiness...

—Henry David Thoreau

I had just settled onto a bar stool in the J. & S. Fish Camp, halfway up the east side of Lake Okeechobee on State Route 98. The "Big Lake" was nowhere in sight. It lay beyond a huge earthen dike which cradle most of its shores to the east, south and west as a flood control measure. The month was March in Florida. It had been a long, warm day.

A middle-aged fisherman next to me at the bar swiveled on his stool, his billed cap tilted back on his forehead. "Did I just see you ride that bicycle into the driveway?" I nodded yes. The bar offered a picture-windowed view of a flagstoned patio with tables, chairs, and a huge outdoor grill with the beckoning aroma of frying fish. However, at the moment, I was more interested in the "Draft Beer" sign at the entrance to the camp than the sizzling fish. It had been a long, hot ride from my home in a western suburb of West Palm Beach.

"Where'd you come from?"

"Royal Palm Beach."

"Why, that's more than 50 miles from here. Give that man a beer!" he called out. The bartender was prompt.

I nodded my thanks, lifted the can to him and drank deeply. I had been sipping tepid water from a plastic bottle on my bike frequently during the long, warm day. That first swallow of the chilled brew seemed to wipe away all that accumulated travel dust, both figurative and literal.

"That a bedroll on the back?" the fisherman asked.

I nodded, but before I could explain what I was up to — that this was my very first bike tour — a waitress passing by stopped long enough to ask me if that was my bicycle leaning on the wall just outside the door.

"Gosh, is it in the way? I'll move it," I replied, beginning to swing off the stool.

"Naw, stay put," she waved. "I saw you ride in and I was just going out to bring you some fried catfish before it's all gone. You looked like you could use some eats."

"Well, thanks," I stammered.

"Whatcha got on the back?" she inquired.

"Oh, a tent and some other stuff. I'm riding around the lake. How much for the fish?"

"Nothin'," she grinned. "It's free for as long as it lasts on late Friday afternoons, but it disappears pretty quick, once it's all fried up and all." I nodded, grinning back and she stepped outside to load up a paper plate. "Enjoy. And have a safe trip," she smiled as she returned with the fish. Before I could slip her a tip for her trouble, she was off to fill someone's order in the crowded lounge echoing with talk of the catches of the day. Lake Okeechobee is known internationally for its bass fishing, but that day there was a lot of talk about perch and crappies, too. The stranger who had insisted on buying my first beer already had ordered another for me.

Word spread from table to table about that guy with the beard at the bar. Apparently a late middle-aged man on a solo cycling circuit of the Big Lake was an unlikely sight, even at the J. & S. camp, where individuality abounds.

More beers appeared before me, unsolicited. I drank them, silently raising a toast to whoever sent them over. These gestures of unexpected fellowship were the first of many I received during my bike trip through nine states. However, nowhere have I been so warmly welcomed by fellow outdoorsmen so instantaneously as was the case on that first day of touring just inland of the shores of Lake Okeechobee.

By the time I had acknowledged all the free beer, wolfed down the free, fried catfish, and had answered questions about my equipment and intentions, the sun had set. Darkness falling on a Friday night usually goes quietly unnoticed in my daily life, but it proved a handicap at the J. & S. I had tried in vain to buy a round or two for those who had gathered at the bar around me, but they all waved me off. The cans kept appearing before me, and I kept thanking smiling strangers as I drank. I didn't realize until it was much too late that setting up camp always should be done before seriously celebrating one's arrival.

As the three-piece string band was tuning up for the evening, I tried to catch the barkeep's eye. He was the one who assigned the camp sites. "Don't worry," the new friend next to me at the bar explained. "He told me where you're to go. It'll be eleven bucks. Look, right there." He pointed through the window and beyond the flagstoned patio. "You'll be right between that RV and the laundry room. See that light burning over the door? The facilities are right there, too."

I nodded. Not precisely what I had envisioned for my first night under the stars on the banks of the Big Lake, but I was not complaining. My campsite was maybe 50 feet from the entrance to the bar. It looked unlike any other "lakeside" campsite I had ever experienced. This parking lot-appearing patch of sand and grass wasn't what I had visualized early that morning as I left my home with *Sir Walter*. Thoreau and his cozy cabin on the shores of Walden Pond flickered for an instant, then was snuffed out. What was that cement slab between my space and the "facilities"? It looked suspiciously like the cover of a septic tank. Behind the slab in the near distance was a weed-strewn canal. The perimeter of its tiny turning basin was dotted with moored boats in slips covered by tin roofs to keep the blazing south Florida sun at bay along with seasonal rain showers.

At that late hour, I was grateful for the indirect light reflecting from the bulbs burning at the entrances to the rest rooms because, even though I had practiced-pitched my extremely light-

3

weight pup tent several times in my own backyard before heading west, I would be sleeping in it for the first time this night. I had been accepting all these congratulatory libations with unrestrained appreciation. "Pitching this mama will be no sweat," I muttered to nobody in particular as I walked the loaded bike to my assigned campsite. *Sir Walter* seemed to be wobbling under his load. Fortunately, the rear corner of the "facilities" building blocked out the bright lights from the bar. I would have a modicum of privacy.

Although the mosquitos weren't too pesky at that late hour, I was grateful for the design of the tiny tent. Its sewn-in floor and attached front and rear flaps, complete with mosquito netting, promised a peaceful, bug free night. Not like the old-fashioned tents of my youth. No pitch poles in this space age baby. Super lightweight tubing was to arch over the roof, supporting the whole thing from the outside. But first, I had to unwrap the mother. I hadn't recalled tying that drawstring at the top of the container bag quite so tightly. Maybe it cinched up on the ride out from West Palm Beach.

I was almost ready to cut the string with my trusty knife when it began to loosen. No sweat now. All I had to figure out was where I had tucked the aluminum stakes. Where had I packed the flashlight?

The entrance light to the facilities helped. Barely. I finally located the stakes. Why, they had spilled out of the container bag and were right there at my feet. I staked out the floor of the tent. It was easy in that sandy soil. Then, it took only two or three tries to assemble the tubes and slip them into their proper pockets fore and aft in the tent's roof portion. I hadn't recalled having so much trouble during the trial runs in my backyard. Must be this strange place. The corner fittings to be inserted into the ends of the tubes at ground level took some concentration. There. All four of them. Now the fly which covered the tubes and extended over the tent. No sweat. Well, just a drop or two until everything was upright. Must be the dim light. Now, lift the loaded saddlebags off the bike and throw them into the other side of the tent, lock the bike to a convenient tree outside, blow up that air mattress, roll out the light-as-a-feather sleeping bag, and climb inside. Simple. Why did it seem to be taking so long?

Once inside, I zipped up the mosquito netting at both ends of the tent. As I fumbled in the dark, I wondered why the nettings had tabbed zippers at both ends of their arched pathways. No, it wasn't the netting. I was zipping both the netting flap and the outer door flap at the same time. Strange. It hadn't been a problem before. No sweat. We seemed all closed up. Nice evening breeze flowing through. No bugs. No sweat. I don't remember falling asleep.

Suddenly I was acutely aware of a piercing call from Mother Nature. I could see the lighted entrance to the public lavatory quite easily through the netting, but I couldn't seem to get the hang of the zippers to open the tent's flaps. As any modern camper knows, tents these days have not only sewn-in floors, but double-zippered flaps and screens as well. Now, one can zip open the flap, leaving the inner netting intact to fend off the stinging creatures hovering outside. The paths the zipper tabs followed were parallel to one another. I zipped open the flap. I discovered one cannot crawl through mosquito netting. Why hadn't the mother opened?

My panic mounted in direct response to urgent signals from my nether regions, increasing as I got to my hands and knees. Moving as quickly as possible, I inadvertently zipped up the outside flap again instead of unzipping the netting inside. One could zip or unzip what seemed an infinite number of combinations, none of which was allowing me to escape before the unthinkable would happen in this modern tent, complete with a sewn-in, waterproof floor.

For an interminable time, I fumbled with those accursed zippers, drawing arcs in the dark from one side of the tent to the other. Still it didn't open. At one desperate moment I had considered slashing the netting and nylon fabric with my knife, but I couldn't find it. Then, I remembered. My knife was outside in a tool kit bag slung under the top tube of my bike's frame.

Now, I was sweating. I was in pain, doubled over. Never before had I felt quite so trapped. I sat back on one haunch, stretching one leg out to one side. It helped. Brows furrowed, I stopped clawing helplessly and selected one zipper tab firmly, and zipped it slowly around the arch, praying. Voilà! The mosquito netting fell away. I reached down and grasped the second zipper tab. The front flap also fell away. I scrambled out on all fours. I had avoided the unthinkable. I was alone, still doubled over, but free! All seemed quiet. I was very grateful for the proximity of the facilities to my campsite.

My post-midnight misadventure answering nature's urgent call sticks more clearly in my memory than any other incident of that very first bike tour.

The four-day trip stretched for only 220 miles, but it launched me into my South Florida-to-Canada adventure. I had been careful in the selection of my wearing apparel, refusing to wear my Lycra-tight pants on The Trip. I didn't want to be mistaken for one of those high-tech, steel-bunned racing types who might, on occasion, weave in and out of traffic, run red lights, or sneak up on the right edge of a long line of traffic stopped at a crossing, then zoom ahead, ignoring all the courtesies. Not me. I wanted to blend right in with everyone else along the way, wearing the local colors and relatively baggy (but strategically padded) shorts.

I discovered on my trip around the Big Lake that folks spotting an older man hunched over a nondescript road bike well over to the right on a highway determined he wasn't any threat to their safety. In fact, they may have been a little worried about *his* safety.

Cycling around Lake Okeechobee was frustrating in only one respect. I never seemed to be at a place at the end of the day where I could camp right on its shores. Its earthen dike blocked any lakeside view from the roads surrounding it except at the northernmost end where the Kissimmee River empties into the Big Lake. However, there was plenty to see as I pedaled *Sir Walter* along Route 441 up the east side of the lake. The rim canal outside the huge dike was clearly visible on my left. It was the passageway for boats like those moored at the J.& S. fish camp up to one of eight locks placed strategically around the Big Lake's perimeter to allow traffic in and out and to control water levels. I was dazzled by flocks of wading birds in the marshy areas. Ducks and coots, cattle egrets, common egrets, purple gallinules, ibis, bitterns, anhingas and majestic blue herons were plentiful. The sight of more than 20 wood storks rising from a roadside marsh as I passed was impressive.

I stopped at Henry Creek on the Big Lake's northeast shoulder long enough to see how one of the boat locks around the Big Lake worked. I was told by the lock tender, B. C. Brewer of Okeechobee City, that the lake was about two feet higher at his lock that day than the surrounding canals and rivers. The lake's level varies, depending upon how hard and from what direction the wind blows. "Wind tides," I was told, can vary the depth as much as two feet from one side of the lake to the other. Mr. Brewer explained that Okeechobee was the largest North American freshwater lake wholly within the borders of any one state. Its average depth is only nine feet.

Later on that second day, I regretted not taking time to visit the Brighton Seminole Indian Reservation on the Big Lake's west side, just north of Lockport, but I was searching for a possible place to camp on Okeechobee's shores. The huge dike spoiled my view to the east as effectively as it had to the west the previous day.

My second night of camping was spent tucked behind the Sunday School section of a church. I was hidden from view along State Road 78. Although I knocked on house doors on either side of the church property to gain permission to pitch my tent, nobody answered. Dusk was descending. I decided to chance a trespass. Rationalizing that churches throughout the ages have offered sanctuary to those needing shelter, I wheeled *Sir Walter* quickly around the back of the church. The only living creatures of any size to investigate my hidden campsite between the church Sunday School building and a pasture were too young heifers. They watched from across two strands of barbed wire fence as I pitched my tent. How easy it was compared to the previous evening! After I had settled in, the cows ambled over to a flock of cattle several hundred yards away.

I had grabbed a couple of sandwiches and a soft drink at a roadside grocery store/gas station before I located my surreptitious campsite. By the time I had spread my ground cloth and pitched my tent, dusk had fallen. How different I felt in that peaceful, ecclesiastical setting — a far pedal (60 miles) from the relatively boisterous, secular setting of the night before. After making certain I would know exactly where I had placed the flashlight and how the tent zippers worked from the inside, I dropped off to sleep on my inflated air mattress. I barely remember my head hitting my rolled-up clothes which served as my pillow. Only an occasional distant lowing of the cattle on the other side of the fence disturbed my slumber. Even my bladder behaved.

Before the sun cleared the eastern horizon the next day, I was "on the road again," wishing I knew the words to that Willy Nelson tune. I did sing the Roger Miller ditty, "King of the Road," over and over to myself as I cycled the roads less traveled by, though I found no "rooms to rent — fifty cents."

On that third day, I visited a riverside park in Moore Haven

VITAMIN SUPPLEMENTS. Ginkgo Biloba for mental alertness, instant yogurt (tasted terrible), Potassium Asporotate to relieve cramping muscles at day's end.

at the southwest corner of the Big Lake. At this gateway from Lake Okeechobee to Ft. Myers via the Cross-Florida Barge Canal stands a huge cypress tree on the shore of the Caloosahatchee River. Local legend has it that the tree saved many a life as folks swept along in the fury of the 1926 and 1928 hurricanes clung to its top branches until the waters receded. More than 2,000 residents living around the Big Lake lost their lives in those hurricanes. These disasters prompted the federal government in 1931 to authorize construction of the dike and locks system around the lake by the U.S. Army Corps of Engineers

As dusk began to fall on what was to be my last night of bike-camping around Lake Okeechobee, I passed John H. Stretch Memorial Park on Route 27. On its east side lay a gravel road which slanted diagonally up the side of the earthen dike. I decided to walk my bike up the road to see if there might be a shore on which to pitch a tent on the other side. Again, I was disappointed. No beach, only limestone outcroppings right to the water's edge. But I pitched my little tent anyway. There was still no view across a calm body of water as one might expect. Instead, the rim canal, dug as the dike was being built more than 60 years earlier, provided a waterway for fishermen's outboard-powered, flat-decked bass boats. Of course, Spanish moss hung down from the towering trees on tiny, uninhabited islands across the rim canal from where I was camped, and there, in the distance, stretched the Big Lake.

By this third night of camping out, I had mastered the zippers routine. As luck would have it, in late afternoon, a Florida Fish and Wildlife officer came driving along the sandy, grassy road on top of the dike and spotted me. He told me I was illegally camped. It was late. I was tired, so I turned on my best imitation of an innocent elder. Could I stay just that one night, then be gone by dawn's earliest light? I now realized how millions of homeless old men have pleaded quietly with law enforcement officers since homelessness began.

"Do you have a weapon?" the game warden inquired. Heavens no, I didn't. They were too heavy to carry. Weight's at a premium on a bike, especially one being pedaled by someone my age. I've come to dislike the title "senior citizen." I prefer "seasoned student," but I didn't stop to explain why as dusk grew deeper that evening. I imagined that city dwellers to the east had heard about those rednecks out around the lake. A rowdy bunch. Untrustworthy, etc., etc.

If you assume the worst about people, chances are you're going to attract some who live down to your expectations. I never carried a firearm. I'm an animal lover who wears a T-shirt stating, "Support the right to arm bears." Yes, I carried a small cylinder on my key ring during the Okeechobee Lake circuit. Its manufacturer claimed its contents, under pressure, could hit someone from 10 feet away if aimed correctly, then paralyze the criminally-inspired culprit for 20 minutes with tear gas and red pepper. But how far would 20 minutes get me on a loaded bike? I'd think twice before I'd use it, and only in dire circumstances. Those crises never have arisen in the more than 2,000 miles I've toured so far. Besides (I didn't blurt this out to the officer), I'm not sure if I could shoot somebody under any circumstances.

He shrugged his shoulders and explained that there were more confrontations between the "Rangers" and the folks who lived right along this section of the lake than in any other place around its perimeter. I was silent, but felt like replying, "Do I look like I'm a uniformed official, threatening to spoil anyone's illegal fun, like fishing or hunting without a license, drinking while driving a boat or just raising a little ruckus on general principles?" The officer's voice jarred me from my musing.

"Get on your way early. I'll swing back to check on you tomorrow, just to make sure," he said as he pulled away.

I broke camp that next day before the morning mist had lifted, cramming tent, fly, ground cloth and miscellaneous clothing into my saddlebags. As was true during most of my other early morning exits from non-designated campsites in various states, I ignored the sometimes dripping dampness of my gear as I packed up, vowing to stop along the way to dry things out after the sun had risen to an appropriate height and strength. It usually offered its rays when I needed them the most.

That particular morning was memorable in another respect. Because the mist was so thick around Lake Okeechobee, I thought I'd ride for awhile along the top of the huge earthen dike which almost surrounded the lake. From forty feet above State Road 27's black-topped level, I could barely see through the ground fog the cars and trucks passing below. The officer who warned he was coming back to check on me was nowhere in sight as I started to ride toward South Bay along the top of the dike. It wasn't easy pedaling. The wet grass soaked my shoes and socks as I pedaled slowly along that seldom-used washboard road in the center of the top of the dike. *Sir Walter's* tires were wider (700x35) than those on racing bikes, but not the "fat-tire" variety so popular on mountain bikes these days. He was having a tough time of it in the sand and grass. [Mountain bike riders might be interested in participating in the annual 110-mile, three-day, dike-top "Big 'O' Bike Ride" on Veteran's Day weekend each year. It was organized two years after my Okeechobee circuit. See Appendix A for details.]

We had struggled, bumping along through the dew-laden grass, for only about a mile when I sighted a long line of sugar cane cutters just beginning to chop through the endless rows of sugar cane in a field on the other side of Route 27 from the Big Lake. Their machetes glinted in the rising morning sun as they bent to their work. Their legs were protected by metal shin guards. For some reason, I thought of ancient Samurai warriors as I watched those muscular, Caribbean islanders swinging their long blades, the cane stalks towering over and tumbling around them. I counted the backs of 127 cane cutters. I was certain their feet were as wet as mine from the dew in the tall grass at that early hour. And I was sure more of their muscles would ache at the end of a day's work than mine would from riding.

I rode another mile, then walked *Sir Walter* diagonally down the road side of the dike to Route 27. By the time I regained the highway from the dike, the cutters had disappeared from view in the dissipating morning mist. I stopped to talk to a young man directing cane-gathering machines across the highway, waving his red flag to halt Route 27 traffic as huge, loaded wagons lumbered across the highway on their way to the crushing mill.

"How many hours a day do they work?" I asked him, nodding toward the disappearing cutters.

"From 7 a.m. 'til 2 p.m. I tried cutting cane one time," he answered quietly. "Just once." He turned away, shaking his head.

On the way back to Royal Palm Beach, I thought quite a bit about those cane cutters. How they would have wondered why an old guy would pedal a bike all that distance just for the fun of it. It had been enjoyable. However, the sheer delight of having almost completed my first honest-to-goodness shakedown cycling cruise was diminishing. I had 38 miles to go, and Old Man Weather was waving his wand, stirring things up.

I encountered the reason for having a combination of 18 different gear ratios along the relatively flat roads of Florida — the wind in one's face. Springtime headwinds are to flatland cyclists what mountain slopes are to those seeking snowcapped vistas. The way to combat head winds and increasingly steeper grades is to gear down. My average speed dropped to seven miles per hour as the wind swept across the open cane and vegetable fields of the Belle Glade area.

My shoulders and neck muscles complained, and the soles of my feet began to burn. However, I knew I'd be home soon. I also knew I could endure and enjoy getting back to nature on a bike. I took my mind off my pain by planning my route north.

Thoreau's memorable adage, "most men lead lives of quiet desperation," crossed my mind. Not my life. Mine was a relatively quiet one, yes, but full of joy and anticipation. Canada, here I come.

CHAPTER TWO

NORTH ALONG THE ATLANTIC

While you are alone you are entirely your own master and if you have one companion you are but half your own, and the less so in proportion to the indiscretion of his behavior.

— Leonardo Da Vinci
Notebooks

Da Vinci's logic spoke to my choice for going solo that sunny May morning as I prepared to leave home in Royal Palm Beach, a village a few miles west of West Palm Beach. I planned to head east to the Atlantic Ocean, then I would turn north. My bike and racks carried 40 pounds of gear. I'd be on the road, self-contained at last. I could go at my own pace, stop anywhere and anytime I chose. Independence personified.

Like most overland bike travelers intend, I had planned to leave just as the sunrise crested the eastern horizon. But I lingered over breakfast with my wife, Kate, realizing that it could be more than a month before we would be together to share a meal again. Besides my four-day trip around Lake Okeechobee, I also had biked the "Across Florida" ride from Belle Glade on Lake Okeechobee's southeastern corner to Punta Gorda on Florida's west coast. Sponsored annually by the West Palm Beach Bicycle Club, the ride totaled 100 miles. Cyclists call them "centuries." I found I could handle long rides as long as I kept my speed between 12 and 15 miles per hour. Now the only unanswered question was, could I pedal a significant distance every day on a fully-loaded touring bike of *Sir Walter's* vintage?

I had undergone a complete physical exam before the upcountry ride, including an Exercise Thallium Stress Test. It was first for me. Those with heart conditions are quite familiar with the test: a moving treadmill with an inclined plane to jog against, and one's chest plastered with wired patches to monitor one's heart performance. As my heart rate was carefully monitored, the treadmill was inclined by degrees until, after ten minutes or so, the machine was halted.

"If you don't make it, you won't have your heart to blame," a nurse told me after the test. I had the feeling that the doctor and the other attendant — as a precaution, the test requires more than one health care professional to stand by as a "patient" takes it — thought I had a mental problem rather than a physical one for planning to ride solo upcountry at 68.

My understanding wife knew how much I wanted to try it, and why I wanted to try it alone. As the weeks of sending for state maps, county maps, special maps from *Adventure Cycling* magazine passed, (see Appendix A) and I gradually gathered gear and supplies, I grew more anxious to be on the road. But I had no idea just how far I could travel each day.

Of special help were the *Atlas* and *Gazetteer* backroad map series published by DeLorme Mapping of Freeport, Maine (see Appendix A). These included maps of Georgia, Tennessee, Virginia, Ohio and Michigan. I also was especially grateful for topographical maps available through DeLorme. These "topo" maps indicate varying elevations of terrain with grey, fine pencil-like lines. The closer together the lines, the steeper the hills or mountains. Together with "local knowledge," the DeLorme series covering Virginia guided me through some of the more challenging passes found in the Appalachians (see Chapter 8).

Most cross-country touring cyclists who travel in groups across America, usually from west to east, average 80 miles a day. However, their personal gear is "sagged" by vans or trucks from one overnight resting place to the next. I was toting my own equipment.

I set no goals for how far I would travel each day. I had told only my wife and my daughter Cindy of my proposed attempt. My other two grown children and Kate's five grown kids knew nothing about the pending adventure. The less said the better until the goal was either reached or I failed to make it all the way. Only time would tell.

Canada was nine states north as that proverbial crow flies. I had chosen to challenge the Appalachian Mountains merely because they were under that fictional, black-feathered flight path. Pt. Huron in eastern Michigan, Cindy's home, was my ultimate destination. It sets on the second knuckle of that state's "thumb." When I arrived in Pt. Huron, I would cycle on to Sarnia, Ontario at the other end of an impressive bridge spanning the St. Clair River. It flows between Lake Erie and Lake Huron. I merely wanted to claim, "I rode from South Florida to Canada." No false modesty for me. Twenty-year old *Sir Walter* proved a valiant courser.

My sexagenarian frame fit him just fine. However, I sensed he resented being loaded down with touring gear. His knightly station did not warrant him being treated as a pack mule. I discovered when I circumnavigated Lake Okeechobee that a loaded touring bike could act rather mulish, too. Not nearly as responsive to sudden changes of direction as it had been when being ridden, er, bareback, so to speak. I quickly learned not to try to turn too sharply left or right.

[Note to would-be self-contained touring cyclists: practice steering a loaded bike before you hit the road. The highway could suddenly hit you back if you turn too abruptly. Cardinal rule: if you accidentally swerve and run off the pavement, steer straight ahead until the bike stops, then walk it back before you mount again.]

I quickly realized as I loaded *Sir Walter* that he might be far more mulish on the upcountry trip because his load was heavier than it was as we circumnavigated the Big Lake. Now I was packing for a month of cycling, not a four-day, round-the-lake jaunt. Strapped atop the rear rack behind me was my pup tent and fly cover, wrapped in a waterproof ground cloth. The bundle also included an air mattress, tightly wrapped in its deflated state, and an inflatable canvas seat/backrest. I thought it would make a comfortable lounge chair at my camp sites. I used it once.

MORNING ROUTINE includes boiling water in one-burner lightweight stove for coffee or tea, instant cereal, checking route planned for day and brushing teeth.

Below my shelter pack, down either side of the rear wheel, I had bolted steel-framed panniers with their saddlebags to the rear wheel frame. They carried a tiny, one-burner stove, nested cooking gear and stainless steel utensils, a blanket, campsite moccasins, a pair of slacks, three T-shirts, a long-sleeved knit sweater, and an extra belt.

I also filled the forward panniers with road maps, miniature 7x20 binoculars, a palm-sized compass, the lightest 35mm camera I could find, color slide film and a cassette recorder and blank audio tapes. I made certain the camera and tape recorder were protected by tucking them into wool socks. Then I wrapped them with shorts, skivvies, a pair of neon yellow leggings, and a water resistant jacket. Also in the front panniers I stored a jackknife, notebooks, a headlamp flashlight, sunblock, washrag, towel, soap in dish, toothpaste, toothbrush, dental floss — the usual first aid stuff, but always the lightest I could find. Oh yes, and a tube of A & D Ointment for that chafed area every questioner asks about: "Didn't your rear end wear out?" More about that later.

I zipped all of these items inside oversized sandwich bags.

Driving rain has a way of soaking through even the most water-proofed of saddlebags.

I deliberately did without a handlebar bag. I wanted to keep *Sir Walter's* center of gravity as low as possible. Some miscellaneous gear wasn't as handy in the front panniers as it might have been in a handlebar bag, but it seemed the wisest way to stow my gear. Almost every touring bicycle also has a small rear pouch, a "clip wedge" under the seat. That's where I carried Allen and box wrenches, screwdrivers, tire levers, and tire and tube patches.

One can also strap on an extra tire under the seat, but I depended on the best 700x35 size road tires I could buy and new, heavy duty tubes. I also added rim tapes, self-sticking plastic wheel liners to help prevent spoke ends from protruding through the rim from the inside. (I was told a sharp bump could drive a spoke into the inner tube from the hub side. I had NO flats in my

CLEAN CLOTHES were managed during the every-third-night stop in motels. Here, wool socks dry in the morning sunlight.

1,668 miles over all kinds of back country, mostly paved roads. I strapped an eight-inch long tire pump under my seat bar; fortunately, I never had to use it.

Everything seemed in tiptop shape, and even though *Sir Walter* was not exactly in his prime (he weighed 40 pounds unloaded), I really felt I was (166 pounds, stripped, I actually gained two pounds on the trip, lots of biscuits and gravy).

To be safe on the road, a cyclist must be seen. This was particularly true for the route I had chosen through the Appalachians from south to north. Cross-country cyclists pass through those ranges occasionally, usually traveling from west to east, but I was heading north. Drivers of cars and trucks in the predominantly rural areas I had designated for my route may not ever have encountered touring cyclists on their roads. Many paved roads were narrow and winding. Hairpin turns in the mountains were commonplace. I wanted to make certain that I would be noticed. To be noticed is to wear the brightest colors.

Kate and I had shopped for the brightest colored fabric we could locate to serve as covers for the rear saddlebags and tent. We discovered a polyester fabric in "Hunter's Orange." Some fabric folks identify it as "Safety Orange." It is commonly used for caps and other wearing apparel by game hunters who don't want to be mistaken for their targets. School crossing guards and other directors of traffic, both pedestrian or vehicular, frequently are clad in Safety Orange.

I also rigged a three-foot long fiberglass wand to my rear wheel rack with a brilliant pink pennant attached to its top. That and the Safety Orange baggage coverings kept me more visible to passers-by, both coming and going. Many a person would comment as I stopped at service stations and country stores along the way, "We could surely see you comin' with your rig covered in that orange stuff and that flag a'wavin." I'd nod happily, knowing my sartorial brilliance was paying off.

As I waved goodbye to Kate, the excitement of finally being on the road all by myself took over. I had no timetables. I could set my own pace. A small computer on my handlebars would keep track of my current speed, my average speed, the distance covered, and the time I was on the road every day. I could stop and stroll on a beach if I felt like it.

Of course I would miss my beloved wife, but I had assured her I would call every other night. If the temperature, terrain or traffic proved too big a challenge for me, she had agreed to drive or fly up to meet me, wherever I happened to be. She knew I was a prudent cyclist, and she has a deep religious faith, too. She chatted lightheartedly about guardian angels and appeared quite composed when I finally left our home that May day.

Many folks who have heard the tale of my upcountry adventure ask me what my wife REALLY felt about the trip. "Did she really let you go ahead with it without an argument?" was a frequent question. Or, "Your wife must have thought you were crazy." Or a rather sad comment, "My wife would never let me do it."

I realize that lots of husbands have over-protective or over-cautious wives. Kate falls somewhere in between. She's also a superb listener. She asks plenty of questions before she gives an opinion. "What route do you plan to take?" How long do you think you'll be on the road?" Will that old bike hold up okay? Have you figured out how much it will cost?"

Kate listened quietly as I tried to tell her what a great adventure I thought it would be. I would have loved to do it with her, but she declined. She is quite healthy, but tends to be less adventuresome than I. I'm blessed with superb health, tend to be enthusiastic, and am a lifelong optimist. Like many, many other older people on relatively fixed incomes, we have to keep close track of our expenses, and that was one of our concerns. No, I wasn't going to buy a new bike. No, I didn't plan to linger along the way. And, yes, I DID realize that spending 30 or so nights in motel rooms would be more than our budget would allow. That's why I had decided to camp out two of every three nights or so, and I would prepare my own by-dawn's-early-light breakfasts. I had even tried to persuade the Quaker Oats Company to sponsor the trip because I would be eating their neatly packaged, individual servings of "just add water and eat" instant oatmeal. I had worked for a year in the public relations department of the company in Chicago way back in 1949. I suggested by letter that Quaker sponsor my upland trip. I was not successful.

I DID get a friendly letter from their marketing director, accompanied by a bunch of packets of instant oatmeal, brightly colored T-shirts advertising Gatorade, and plenty of packs of that sports drink in powder form. However, the marketing director politely informed me that, as far as "name recognition" was concerned, they had chosen Michael Jordan to promote their products. I could understand that. Kate and I had a good laugh over my alleged claim to be effective promoting the virtues of instant cereal and a sports drink along the way through Appalachian back roads.

As I explained my plans, my attentive wife listened. What a treasured gift that is for any spouse, to always have a friendly ear nearby. Kate had listened once before about a small, solo, sea-going adventure I had planned seven years before when I was a mere 61. Long before we had met and married in 1981, I had been a licensed smallboat captain. I had crossed the Gulf Stream between Florida and the Bahamas 62 times in small sailboats with auxiliary engines.

Brian Quinn, a friend of mine in South Florida who was a superb small boat designer and builder, created a two-part, 12-foot rowing-sailing dinghy in 1981. When not bolted together amidships, the bow section of this unique boat could nest inside the stern section and be stowed on a larger yacht. Its ability to track while being rowed or sailed was remarkable for a dinghy its size. I wanted one. Brian had built several of them, but they were pricey. I suggested that I row and sail (as need be) one of the first boats to be popped out of its fiberglass mold from Palm Beach to the Bahamas and back. Then, I'd write a story about its sea-going properties. My fee for the publicity would be to keep the dinghy. Its maker had agreed, but when I had attempted the Gulf Stream crossing, the mini-voyage had not gone as planned. This was on my mind that last morning before I left on another mini-odyssey.

Kate began to grin as I was revealing my plans for my nine-state bicycle tour. I would return to Florida via Amtrak. Kate began to chuckle.

"What?" I asked, puzzled.

"Well, at least I won't have to drive up to Cape Canaveral to bring you back home," she said. The Cape is more than 100 miles north of our home.

"Nope, I guess not," I smiled. She was reminding me of the ill-fated Gulf Stream crossing in the sailing dinghy. The winds had been light and variable and unusually tranquil. The Stream of that 1986 August had swept me north of the Bahamas. I had no choice but to turn west and head for Florida's mainland. I rowed ashore at Cape Canaveral after 59 hours aboard the dink. Kate and her friend, Jane, drove from West Palm to the Cape to pick me up. We car-topped the dinghy back home.

"You know," Kate explained, "I figure you know as much about bicycle touring as you do about sailing. You were able to handle yourself okay then. Why not now? Besides, you'll have road maps and won't be at the mercy of winds, tides, and currents."

That was the end of our discussion about whether she would be comfortable with my upcountry trip. I am indeed fortunate to have such a partner as Kate.

As I write these words, she reads me a letter to a newspaper "advice" columnist from a woman who complains because her husband, now retired, insists on knowing what she plans to be doing every moment they are apart. "Thank goodness we know how important enjoying our own space is," Kate states. "I know you'll keep in touch by phone, and I've got plenty to keep me busy while you're gone. As that sports shoe manufacturer says, "'Just do it!'"

And that was that.

Perhaps what she wrote in a note she sent me toward the end of my trip upcountry explains how she feels about our relationship. She sent it to Cindy's home, and I read it as soon as I had arrived. The message, in its entirety, read, "Frank, Dear, once we

21

are on our right path in life, miracles happen. Meeting you was one of mine. I love you. Kate." Of, course, the feeling is mutual.

My final act of preparation had been filling two plastic bottles with fresh water. They each contained almost a quart of liquid, and were carried in "bottle cages" fastened to my bike's down tube and seat tube. Drinking enough liquids on a long trip is extremely important. How much is enough? I drank two gallons of water on that first warm May day on the road. I covered 73 miles.

That first day, I took the nearest route to the ocean I could find. Along Florida's east coast, one can drive a car or pedal a bike within an echo of the waves pounding the shore, except where inlets cut through barrier islands off the mainland. Then, seaside travelers must turn west to Interstate Highway 1, cross a bridge across the Intercoastal Waterway along a particular inlet and come back east to the barrier island nearest their route.

Those who have traveled along the Atlantic Ocean in Florida from the Georgia line to Miami catch only occasional glimpses of the majestic waves curling onto the beaches. Those barrier islands are aptly named. They undoubtedly protect the real estate developments, commercial businesses and private homes along that coast with their dunes, but they do not offer many vistas of the sea from roads nearest the salt water.

And so these behind-the-dunes shoreline roads are usually less traveled. An orange-studded touring cyclist can be spotted from a tolerable distance away and avoided. Also, at 12 miles per hour, this cyclist could quickly stop when the mood struck him, lean his burdened two-wheeler against a tree or bush and climb a path, staired or not, over the dunes to replenish his soul with a view of the ocean. Sure beats careening along the interstate in a motorized vehicle. And don't forget — you can't beat the miles per gallon.

The sun was setting as I turned inland to Ft. Pierce from the shore road, determined to cross the South Beach bridge over the Intracoastal Waterway on Seaway Drive. Its fixed span rose more than 60 feet above the waterway, allowing all but the larger sail-boats to pass underneath with their fixed masts. I was hot and tired. I was anxious to find a motel rather than camp out that first night. Shifting into my lowest gear, I struggled up the bridge, determined not to walk the bike if I could help it within full view of the flowing vehicular traffic moving homeward in the gathering dusk.

"Why this is just a bridge," I mumbled to myself. "We're going to ride through mountains for gosh sakes. Come on, legs!" It was the longest bridge I had ever crossed on a bicycle. When I reached its center, I stopped, pretending to be enjoying the disappearing sun to the west. I was really trying to get my quads to stop burning before I coasted down the other side. I also wanted to uncramp my hands to make certain they could squeeze the handbrakes as I descended. A loaded touring bike could gather alarming momentum, and I wasn't about to suffer a cycling mishap in my very first day on the road.

I also realized most bridges are not cyclist-friendly. They are narrow. They have curbs along their sidewalks. There's only one direction to travel — straight ahead. No room to maneuver.

UNINTENTIONALLY HUMOROUS sign? Do they really accept crickets and worms for payment? Local offbeat signs and slogans along the way added to the adventure.

Cyclists go with the flow. They have no choice. I don't remember much of any descent from the crest of any bridge I crossed anywhere on a bike. My pounding heart drowned all memories. One proceeds as fast as one can, and always sighs with relief when one levels out on the other side.

The roadside motel that night on the west side of U.S. 1 heading north was memorable only because it seemed as cramped inside as a steep bridge is intimidating outside. But rooms were only $25, and my budget was tight. The cars parked before the units were of *Sir Walter's* vintage, it seemed. I was so grateful for a bed I didn't notice that the bathroom faucets — both of them — dripped, and my air conditioning unit was stuttering. Late that night the a/c quit entirely, and all the windows were sealed shut. The steady drip, drip, drip of the bathroom faucet seemed to be amplified beyond tolerance. I vowed to camp out the next night. Fresh, cool, night air should never be taken for granted. That next evening, my wish was realized, but Mother Nature added an unanticipated gesture. Camping out, like crossing bridges, has some uncertain moments.

CHAPTER THREE

PERCH BONES AND PLACES
TO PERCH

"A fine and pleasant misery"

—Patrick E. McManus

As I pedaled away from that cheerless motel on the north end of Ft. Pierce on the second day of my upland solo cycling tour, I vowed to stay as far away from man-made accommodations as possible. "Tonight, I'll find me one of those sylvan glens the poets rhyme verses about and pitch my pup tent," I muttered. Little did I realize how that apt phrase by Patrick McManus, the dean of outdoor humorists, when he referred to tent camping in the Good Old Days would resonate so acutely. It echoed all around me on the first night I camped out on my way north. It wasn't that I lacked the proper equipment. It was Mother Nature's generous baptism that night. "Total immersion" took on a whole new meaning.

The day began fair enough. As the sun backlighted low-hanging cumulus clouds on the eastern horizon, I was on the road again. I decided to stay on U.S. 1, a primary link between the Northeast and Florida as the "Interstate" era dawned during the 1930s. I could catch glimpses of the Intracoastal Waterway by riding on its west side instead of heading north on its east side, where, again, I would be tucked away from a view of the sea by sand dunes.

I had applied a dab of A & D Ointment to the slightly burnished areas of my rear end before leaving the motel. It was more a preventative measure than a medicinal treatment. I had discov-

25

ered on my Big Lake circuit, back when I was still making minor adjustments to my saddle post, that the height of one's bicycle saddle is a key factor to preventing one's tush from becoming too tender. How high you sit is critical for comfort and efficient pedaling.

Usually, beginning cyclists choose to keep their seats low to feel safer. To be able to flip their feet from the pedals to the ground for total support in case of sudden stops is more important than pedal power. School-age bikers, while commuting or in socializing modes to and from school or around their neighborhoods, tend toward lower saddles on easily maneuverable frames and wheels. They're not concerned with energy-efficient riding. If they were, they would raise their saddles to the proper height. The balls of one's feet should be at the center of the pedals. As a pedal reaches its lowest position, the thrusting leg should be almost fully extended.

A bike racer or tourer knows these things which I had to learn. Keep your foot parallel to the road. Beware of dropping your heel as you stretch for the proper downthrust at the most extended point of your leg. If your knee is slightly bent as you bottom out, you've got it right. This also prevents your rear end from sliding from side to side as you pedal. A hardly perceptible lateral motion can lead to major discomfort over a full day of riding, especially in warm weather. The idea is not to lubri-

ONE OF my games along the way. This is as far away as I could pedal from a camera with a delayed shutter release on the way to Damascus, Virginia. You know what they say about "All work and no play..."

cate your moving parts to prevent friction, but to keep your butt as immobile as possible as you pedal.

As you try out a particular saddle height, also make sure that the seat is level, fore and aft. The trick is to carry your weight evenly on the area between the two lowest orifices you possess. If the bike's seat is too high, friction can develop in that central area, the perineum, the weight-bearing ridge. It should not be moving from side to side when you pedal.

Of course, male and female anatomies differ — viva la difference! — so saddle contours vary accordingly. It has to do with the "perch bones" (ischial tuberosities for the technically inclined) of your pelvis. These two bumps on either side of the pelvic bones, covered with muscle and fatty padding, are your seat cushions, so to speak. Women's perch bones are usually farther apart than men's, so designers and manufacturers of bicycle seats take these anatomical facts into consideration. Hank Martin, in his bike touring book, *Follow the White Line*, delves deeply into perch bones.

Sir Walter's saddle startles people at first. It has no padding. Known as a "Brooks" saddle, its manufacturer's name, it is made of three-sixteenths-inch thick cowhide. No springs, no padding. "Why, that's hard!" curious folks exclaim, testing it with a forefinger.

"But look at it closely," I suggest. "See those two dents? That's where my perch bones sit." I explain that it takes about one hundred miles of steady riding to break in a Brooks properly. But once it's broken in, you have a custom saddle which keeps chafing to a minimum. The key to comfort is weight distribution. Many touring cyclists prefer a leather saddle. Not only do my perch bones fit just right, but the forward end of my lower anatomy fits, too. Its bony end is my pubic arch. The "horn" of my bicycle seat is shaped to accommodate that male arch. It's more curved, as in an inverted V, than is a female pubic arch. That's why touring saddles come in so many shapes and sizes. Depends upon one's gender, dimensions and preference.

Pedaling a bike for ten hours, with ten-minute stretching

pauses every 15 miles or so, and a break for lunch, is not at all uncommon for serious touring bike riders. My back didn't ache nearly as much as if I'd been sitting on a car seat driving for that length of time.

I did make one mistake that second day as the heat waves began to shimmer in my line of sight ahead on the highway's asphalt. I lingered too long over my second glass of iced tea at lunch in an air-conditioned restaurant. As I rose from my stool at the counter, a cramp grabbed my left quad, the top leg muscle between the knee and the hip. I tried to ignore it, limping over to the cash register with my check, but a knot was beginning to form in the muscle. I dropped the bill on the counter and rubbed my thigh, hard. The knot dissolved. After that, I learned not to sit in one position too long after an extended ride, especially in an air-conditioned place. Ten minutes off the saddle, walking or stretching, is long enough. Longer rests should be accompanied by gentle massaging. At the end of a day, the massage can be enhanced by the application of oil or salve designed for easing sore muscles.

As the day dimmed, I noticed it was not merely the falling sun which drew a curtain of gloom across the sky. Rain clouds had gathered. A spring cold front was moving through the area from the northwest to the southeast. I was pedaling through Melbourne, 50 miles north of Fort Pierce. My plan was to turn east the next day to see if I could pedal past the Kennedy Space Center along the ocean, 30 miles to the north, but where to pitch my tent that night was my immediate concern.

Darkness was falling fast, and raindrops began to pepper the pavement as I turned into the Wickham County Park in Melbourne. The park ranger in charge was out and about the premises, so *Sir Walter* and I huddled under the eaves outside the ranger's locked office door as the rain pelted down. He finally returned. I registered and plunked down my $16, the fee needed to pitch my tent in the "primitive area" of the park for the night. As soon as he pointed out my numbered site on the map of the park, I headed out into the teeming downpour.

MORNING AFTER first camping night in Melbourne, Florida where I pitched the tent in pouring rain and total darkness, and I literally bailed it out with a wool sock!

I couldn't wait for the torrent to let up because the last light of day was vanishing. I had to make several turns along the paths to get to my assigned spot, and could barely make out the arrows directing me. Lightning flashes helped. I noticed several tents, all larger than mine, pitched near my own site. Although the ground everywhere was now thoroughly soaked, the sandy soil didn't hold the water long. There was some high ground.

I hadn't bothered to dig out my rain gear, figuring I'd have the tent up in a jiffy. The rain was warm, but the wind whipped up the deluge, rippling the puddles *Sir Walter* and I were churning through. Despite the sandy soil, more puddles were beginning to form at the front of my tent site, facing the road. Second-growth pine trees dotted the area. They waved a wet hello as I leaned the bike against one and tried to untie the bungee cords holding my tent and its fly to the rear rack. I figured I'd get them up first, then throw the saddlebags inside the tent and sort things out later.

By the time I had spread out the ground cloth and staked out the tent over it, all daylight had disappeared. The downpour still persisted. Rain hissed on puddles all around me, but the sudden gusts of wind had subsided somewhat. The pine trees dotting the area didn't sway quite so menacingly as when I had first entered the area, but I was soaked through. I finally got the aluminum arch poles assembled in place over the tent and hoisted the external roof hooks to them, groping in the pitch dark and blinding rain. I laughed out loud as I unzipped the front door and mosquito netting, remembering how I had struggled to get them open during my first night of camping with *Sir Walter* on the Lake Okeechobee tour. I was clear-headed, not beer-befuddled now, but rain was running off my nose like an outside leak on a faucet.

I did take time to lock the bike to a tree after throwing the saddlebags inside the tent. There were other tents around me. Some had lanterns shining dimly through them. Not a soul in sight, of course, in the downpour. Fortunately, the rain was warm. I threw the loaded saddlebags into the tent as quickly as possible, and ducked in, zipping up the front door behind me. But what was that dripping behind me, inside the tent?

I turned around in the pitch dark, groping. I was wrist deep in water! Where had it come from? I fumbled for a flashlight, found it and flicked it on. I then learned Rule Number One: Always zip up both ends of your tent before packing it away after a night's camping. You'll never know what the next night will bring. I had neglected to zip up the flap covering the netting at the rear "window" of the tent before I packed it for the upcountry trip. Rain had been pouring into the rear opening while I was busy unloading *Walter* and securing him for the night. My waterproof ground covering and the sewn-in tent floor helped create an instant indoor wading pool. I zipped up the rear flap, knees awash in the puddle.

Stripping off my shoes and wool socks, I began scooping water up with one shoe. Although the doormat-sized pool was an inch deep behind me, the front of the tent seemed to be on slightly higher ground. In my haste, I also had not stretched the fly over the tent. As any tent camper knows, when you touch the roof during a rainstorm, it will begin to leak. My head had been grazing the inside of the pup tent roof constantly as I paddled around trying to keep my gear away from the gathering pool under me. Fortunately, my tiny flashlight was still water resistant. I sloshed out of the tent into the downpour and located the fly. How pleasant was the sound of the rain pattering down on it when I finally got it stretched over the tent and staked down!

Now, how to cope with the mini-pond inside? I had no four-wheeled vehicle to climb into for shelter. The rain-filled night was before me. I had to figure out some way of making my light-weight shelter habitable. Was this a tenting first, bailing out from the inside, scooping up the water with one's shoe, then turning slowly so as not to spill it before one poured it out the front door of the tent into the downpour? I held the flashlight in my teeth during the process (it kept me from waking the neighboring campers with my curses). Any wonder why the name "Poseidon" kept running through my head?

Gradually, the pond diminished to a pool, then to a puddle. My jaw was aching from clenching my teeth around the flashlight when I suddenly remembered a "going tour-

THE MAN in this photo, Kevin Taylor, biked across the U.S. in 1976. His son (Ian) wanted to sit on my bike. Kevin and his wife, Ruth (also shown), are physicians in Mount Dora, Florida. An example of friendly folks all along the route. (See page 40-41)

31

ing" present from some experienced friends of ours. I dug into my dripping packs and found my new headlamp. It was a modern version of a miner's light, but lighter, battery-operated, and complete with an adjustable headstrap. I'd recommend it for all who struggle in soaking pup tents in the dark.

When the puddle became manageable, I switched from bailing with the shoe to sponging with my wool socks. I heartily recommend wool socks to touring cyclists. They not only keep one's feet dry while cycling and tend to keep them cooler in warm climes by "wicking" the heat from burning feet, but they also make excellent bailing sponges of a sort. In no time at all, I had sopped up the remaining water with my wool socks and squeezed them outside the door unto the sandy ground. The rain had diminished, but continued to drizzle for most of the night.

Blowing up my air mattress was not easy while crouched inside the tent, but it made the difference between sleeping on a very damp floor or enjoying relative comfort atop an inch of compressed air captured inside closely-sewn ribs running head to toe. I removed my soaking clothes and changed into damp ones, thankful that I was in humid, springtime south Florida rather than coming across the high mountain passes of the far West. Come to think of it, getting caught in a late spring snowstorm might have been more fun.

I fell asleep with my head on a pillow of rolled, damp T-shirts to the cozy chorus of raindrops above me. At least, contrary to the song, they weren't falling on my head.

CHAPTER FOUR

WIND, SAND AND TIME

**Nature, with equal mind
Sees all her sons at play;
Sees man control the wind,
The wind sweep man away.**

— Matthew Arnold
Empedocles on Etna

When I first became interested in riding a touring bike in south Florida, I asked Joseph McColly, genial owner of the Bicyclery in West Palm Beach, why he offers bicycles for sale with such a variety of gears. The least expensive have three. The most expensive have 21. After all, I inquired, Florida is quite flat, for the most part. Why do we need so many?

"The wind takes the place of hills down here," Joseph replied. I recalled his explanation during the last three and one-half days I struggled to reach the Florida state line and cross into Georgia. A norther blew through the state as I pedaled along U.S. 1 near Ormond Beach. Without my lower gears to help me spin effectively against the brisk breeze, I might have given up the adventure, then and there. Exhaustion kills desire.

The cold front had moved through during a mid-May night while I was tenting in the Tomoka State Forest, north of Ormond Beach. I had managed to start a small campfire after a supper of canned stew. I had warmed my one-dish meal over my tiny stove's one burner. No other campers were in sight as the darkness fell heavily around me. The circle of firelight was comforting, but campfires, to be properly appreciated, require more than one pair of eyes staring dreamily into the flicker of flames.

However, I enjoyed the solitude of that state park far more than the traffic noise which permeated the Crystal Campgrounds

33

near Mims where I had pitched my tent the night before. The small RV park was much too close to Interstate 95, but my need for a night's sleep after a long, hot day's ride swayed my judgment. I had arrived just before sunset. The waning light would cut short a proper search for a site in the wild, so to speak. I opted for peace of mind, paid the fee, and awoke to the heavy whine of car and truck tires several times that night.

Tomoka, on the other hand, was tranquility itself. Only the whisper of the wind through pine needles would accompany my dreams that night. When the rain began, I zipped up the tent netting and, from my sleeping bag, elbows propped, I watched the fire gradually drown. Few informal meditations are more conducive to a great night's sleep, especially with raindrops pattering directly overhead with the wind's whispers outside. Sometime during the night I heard something topple from the nearby picnic table to the ground. I figured a gust of wind had blown the empty stew can and a bottle half full of orange soda to the ground. When I spied raccoon tracks under the table the next morning, the mild mystery was solved. I made a mental note to secure all my garbage under the weighted cover of the proper container nearby before I left my campsite in the morning.

The rain during the night hadn't dampened my plans for a cup of hot coffee. One flick of a match ignited the friendly hiss of blue-flamed white gas from the single burner of my tiny stove. Less than a minute was required to bring a tin cupful of water to a boil. Coffee bags come in handy on a bike tour. Dry cereal — I preferred the individual packets of Instant Quaker Oats with Cinnamon — laced with instant milk (made from dried solids and canteen water) topped with banana slices knocked the edge off my appetite. I'd stop in midmorning somewhere up the line for restaurant pancakes.

Sir Walter and I felt the invisible palm of the wind's hand thrust against us once more as we geared up for the morning's ride. I should say, "geared down" because that north wind's might insisted upon it. One quickly shifts into the easiest spinning gear to keep moving smoothly along. Keep too much pres-

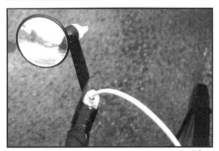

REAR VIEW mirrors are essential for spotting approaching traffic. Not necessarily an exciting photo, but it demonstrates a key piece of equipment, as I can see a truck coming up behind me.

sure off your knees. Remember, you're going to pedal for most of the day. Those silent admonitions were almost subconscious on the road north. Daily riding rhythms depended on the wind's direction and strength, how rested one felt from the previous night's sleep, and road conditions. Of course, traffic was a factor, too.

On this particular mid-week morning, traffic on U.S. 1 was not a problem. However, I was determined to camp on the sea's edge that night. Here I was riding along the coast of my home state, the one with the longest continual, connected, salt-watered coastlines of any in the U.S.A. I had been on the road four days and had yet to camp on the sea's edge. Tonight was the night.

All day I bent to my riding task against that north wind. At noon, a roadside restaurant's radio weather broadcast reported gusts up to 30 miles per hour. At first I was disgruntled. My handlebar computer was ticking off turtlelike speeds of seven to nine miles per hour as we toiled against that relentless north wind. The overcast sky helped in the morning, but as the day passed, the sky cleared and the sun beat down in silent concert to the whistling wind.

Motorists whizzing by were oblivious to that mighty natural force whirling about them. Of course I preferred my bike pedals to their gas pedals. No problem passing emission tests for me, and you can't beat the miles per gallon on a bike. Bike riders are not the culprits who create the dark clouds over Los Angeles, Denver and all the other large cities across the country where air pollution is a truly serious problem. And I'd put up my 68-year-old heart for comparison to any old motorist's heart. When they stepped from their cars after a long drive, they had nothing to be proud of except time saved. But who had decided that time saved by high speeds really was of any benefit if the very air one breathed placed one's lungs in jeopardy?

Wasn't the whole concept of time manmade? Did God enable us to "tell" time via that rolling sun overhead so that we could "keep" it in ever cleverer ways until we could clock it in milliseconds, yea, nanoseconds? Has dividing up time into billionths benefited us all that much? I smiled as I realized I was becoming, intellectually, a conservative, grumpy old man as I bent to my spinning that day. But from then on, I didn't glance at my computer any more except to see how far I had come each day. How long it took was not my prime concern. I would not allow our human obsession with time lost to intrude upon my mini-odyssey any longer.

I was tired when I came upon the Grenada RV campgrounds south of Marineland at suppertime. The site had seen better days. RVs and singlewide trailers dotted the grounds. Some appeared to be semi-permanently settled into their sandy sites. Only one other tent was pitched. Huddled behind an RV, it was blue, family-sized, and braving the gusting wind sweeping across the area. Pounding surf echoed from the campground's front yard, so to speak. A range of pockmarked rocks kept the spindrift from blowing across the designated spaces for temporary residences.

I requested an overnight site closest to that beckoning surf. The owner lifted his eyebrows ever so slightly as he surveyed my loaded bike, shrugged, stated, "Twenty-two dollars," and pointed out the assigned space. What a contrast to two nights before, when I staked out my pup tent during a freshwater downpour in an already drenched site at that county-sponsored campground in Melbourne. Or the very night before, amid the towering pines in the tranquil Tomoka State Forest. Never mind. I wanted to fall asleep just once with the surf echoing in my ears. I would get my wish tonight. I resisted walking up to the dune and the rocky shore beyond it to gaze on the churning sea.

Staking down the tent was almost second nature by now.

The aluminum stakes — thirteen in all — would be sunk deep into the sand by hand. I was next door to an RV. I choose to move up to the seaside edge of my assigned space as far as I was permitted. The crashing surf on the other side of the protecting rocks tossed a thin saltwater spray over the dune in front of me. The wind, by now edging around to the northeast, blew it slantingly back over the dune. Yes! Real salt air! That slight spindrift of sand mixed in would be tolerated.

After I had all the tent stakes buried almost out of sight into the sand, I hooked the tent to its metal arches. Its unzipped flaps fluttered in the wind until I had them properly zipped. Now the arches swayed in the wind. They would settle down once I had the fly up over them. I opened the fly to the wind. It snapped and crackled until I got it stretched and staked over the tent. The arches underneath stopped vibrating somewhat, but they did play a merry tune, taut against the breeze. Great. Music of the sea.

I threw all my gear into the tent, to weight it down just in case it decided to take off. The weight helped settle the vibrating somewhat. Tent and fly seemed to hum a little less. I was all ready to crawl inside to sort out my belongings when a half-grown girl appeared at my elbow. She was, maybe, twelve. Blond. Windblown. Wearing faded bluejeans and a too-large T-shirt listing past Grateful Dead concerts. Surely a hand-me-down.

"Want to see our new kittens?" she asked, thrusting two wriggling, butterscotched fur balls up to me.

"Sure," I said, wondering how long she had been standing there. I accepted the mewing mites, and dropped to one knee to give them some solid sand to struggle in. I turned my back to the wind to shelter them.

"Where's your car?" the girl asked.

"It's at home. In West Palm Beach."

"Well, where's your wife? I noticed that ring on your left hand."

"Well, she didn't feel like taking a bike ride with me."

"Oh, then she can use the car while you're gone?"

"Well, I guess so, but it's a stick shift. She likes hers better. It's automatic."

"You mean you've got two cars?"

"Yep."

By now she was squatting beside me. We were playing with the kittens between us. Three younger kids had sidled up. I smiled over at them, but they looked up at the girl for some sign before they would grin back. She ignored them.

"Did you say two cars."

"That's right."

"And you're riding a bike?"

"Well, yes."

"How far?"

"Well, to Canada." Her expression remained quizzical. She didn't react like adults did when they posed the same question.

"To where?" they'd say, eyes opening wider, and they'd make some other remark, depending upon their age. Younger adults might say, "Cool." Older ones might just shake their heads.

The maybe 12-year-old remained silent concerning my ultimate destination.

"Why are you going that far?"

"Oh, I don't know. It's a challenge for somebody my age, I guess. And my oldest daughter lives in Michigan."

She didn't respond for a moment. The kids, including one rather ragged toddler, had edged in. They began to argue about who was playing with what kitten.

"Hush up," she ordered. They hushed.

After a thoughtful moment she swept up the kittens at our feet and turned toward the battered singlewide immediately behind the RV. Assorted rusting kids' bikes leaned against its unpainted sides.

"Come on, you all," she commanded. "We got to git cleaned up for supper. Mom'll be home soon. She promised she'd bring pizza from work." Then she turned back. "You mean you got two cars and you're riding this old bike?"

38

I nodded, knowing that no explanations would help.

She headed back to their mobile home, sweeping her wind-blown hair from her eyes. She herded the younger children together, juggling the mewing kittens from one hand to the other as she pushed away the children's outstretched arms.

"Wait 'til we git out of this wind," she directed. She looked back once at the fluttering pup tent and shook her head. I turned to get my shaving kit and toothbrush out of one of the front panniers and headed for the public rest room area.

Later that night, after I had ridden against the northeast wind two miles to an ocean front motel/restaurant for a seafood dinner, I crawled back into my flapping pup tent. For a long time, I listened to the surf pounding against the rocks. It would have been perfect except for the wind. That tent flapped and snapped like sheets on a clothesline. As tired as I was, I couldn't get to sleep. Finally, about midnight, I crept out of the tent and moved the whole, trembling thing back behind the battered singlewide. Out of the wind, the tent behaved. I didn't wake until after dawn.

I hurriedly pulled up stakes, packed the salt-scoured tent and fly and crammed them into their bags, shaking off the sand as best I could. The surf still pounded, but I didn't even bother to walk up to the dune to watch the sea crashing against the pock-marked limestone known as "coquina" before I left the oceanside site. It was the last time I would camp near the sea. Oh, I'd pitch my pup tent on the beach one day, but not on this trip. I'd be heading northwest, diagonally inland from now on.

As I pedaled north along A1A with the sun rising higher over my right shoulder, I thought about that young girl, her siblings and the kittens. I smiled about her parting remark the night before — "You mean you got TWO cars and you're riding this old bike?" Nobody else along the way so far had commented on *Sir Walter*'s seemingly road-weary appearance. So his 20-year-old frame's green paint was scratched and chipped in places. So the spokes on his wheels didn't sparkle as they turned in the morning sunshine. His spirit remained as high as mine, I was sure. And I was soon to forget all about the wind-whipped, rather forlorn trailer park as I stopped for breakfast along A1A, more than a dozen miles up the ocean-hugging highway.

"Who does that bicycle out there belong to?"

I looked up from my cup of coffee. I was sitting at the bar of the Pirate's Cove restaurant, all alone in the room. I waved at a 30s-something man coming into the otherwise empty dining room. I had already ordered pancakes and a couple of eggs, over easy. "I'm the guy. Is the bike in your way? I'll move it."

"Heck, no. I just want to buy you breakfast." He strode into the room, followed by a little boy and two women. One held an infant in her arms.

"I'm Kevin Taylor. He extended his arm toward the others." My wife, Ruth. Our friend, Illiana, and my two kids. This is Ian, my son, and the baby's Orion, my daughter." The Taylors were on a weekend vacation from Mount Dora, Florida.

"Very nice to meet all of you, but why buy..."

"Come over here and sit with us," he interrupted, as they settled around an empty table in the dining area. "I'll explain."

I carried my cup and saucer over and joined them. What a contrast to the last person I had talked to — that young girl in the trailer park. With a proud grin lifting his face, Mr. Taylor, bursting with enthusiasm, explained. "I rode a bike across the country during the Bicentennial in 1976. I took time off from college. I'll never forget it. Where are you headed?"

"For Canada. Up through the Appalachians. I live in West Palm Beach. Did you leave from Missoula?"

He nodded yes. "Canada, eh? Sounds like a great trip. Yep, I was with one of the first groups of riders to leave from Montana." We chatted on through breakfast. I had read about the beginnings of organized bicycle rides from the west to the east coast in the mid 70s. After that summer of celebrating our nation's 200th birthday, cross-country cycling blossomed. More than 10,000 cyclists have crossed the country since then. The original Bike Centennial magazine in Missoula developed into Adventure Cycling, a premier bike touring magazine and combined bike-touring business.

Almost 20 years later, Kevin Taylor was describing his adventures with just as much gusto as I imagined he had generated as a long-haired college boy from the Age of Aqarius, cycling along, carefree from college, a temporary dropout.

"You know, it seems like yesterday," he smiled. "You'll never forget it. To Canada, huh? I wish I was going with you."

"I wish you were, too," I smiled, but glancing at his brood, I was happy that I had all that child-rearing behind me. As we left the restaurant together, he lifted his son up into *Sir Walter's* saddle and I snapped a picture of the group. Thanking him again, I waved goodbye. My, that warm-hearted family was quite a contrast to the rather sullen, rag-taggle trailer-dwellers I had chatted with the evening before. Just as they left, Kevin handed me his card. "Keep in touch," he reminded me. As they left, I read the card. Both of them were practicing physicians in Mt. Dora.

That day I still was forced to pedal directly into the northeaster until after I had passed through St. Augustine, Florida's oldest city (1565). As I crossed the Bridge of Lions over the Intracoastal on Anastasia Boulevard, I was able to turn north by northwest and the wind's relentless might seemed to lessen somewhat. I wondered how the bridge got its name. A "lion"? Perhaps the Castillo de San Marcos Fort, a National Monument looming up ahead, would hold the answer to that question.

Waves offshore, whipped by the persistent northeast wind, were breaking in the surf. Turning west on Route 16, I glimpsed the top of a 208-foot stainless steel cross to the south. It marks the Mission of Nombre de Dios where the first Mass in the New World was given in 1565. The towering Christian religious symbol marks the site where the first cross was planted. At last the wind was at my back. Marshlands and cattle pastures beckoned on either side as I rode inland to escape the final ravages of the northeaster.

Crossing the Shands Bridge over the broad St. Johns River, I headed north up its west side, moteling it the next night, shaking the sand out of the tent and fly before settling in to air-conditioned sleeping inside a Green Springs Cove motel. No pounding surf, only the occasional whine of tires along the pavement outside the window.

On the eighth day out of West Palm, I finally crossed the state line into Georgia via Route 301. It had been the original U.S. 1, the first north-south interstate highway in the nation. Now it was almost a back road. I liked it that way.

My tent site on that gentle Georgia night was deep within a pine tree farm north of Folkston. The moon was full. I decided not to pitch the fly over the tent. Clear skies had prevailed all that day. I selected a level area far back from the road between a row of pine trees towering thirty feet about me as far as my eyes could see in every direction.

I sensed that rain would not intrude. I was right, but the moon presented a rather eerie problem. I awoke with a start sometime after midnight. Moonglow was everywhere. My ultra-light tent fabric allowed it to filter through, bathing me. I could almost read by it, right through the fabric. I felt I was in kind of a natural bathtub, naked, with the trees looking down on me, resentful of my intrusion into their sanctuary. The feeling actually kept me awake for some moments. The wind was a mere hush through the trees overhead, and only an occasional gritty murmur of tires on asphalt in the distance disturbed Nature's caress. Gradually I fell asleep in her arms. The trees had forgiven me. No stinging, sandy spindrift that night. Sleeping outdoors in temperate climes is like making love — it's all good; some's just better than others.

Chapter Five

Detours, Birdsong and Swimming Holes

**I will make you brooches and toys for your delight
Of birdsong at morning and starshine at night.**

— Robert Louis Stevenson
Songs of Travel

Nobody likes a demanding detour, unless it's by choice. If it is an unexpected road repair blocking your intended travel path or a physical or mental obstacle keeping you from a goal of much wider dimensions, it chills. If you choose to take one, it thrills. I had both kinds on the road.

I faced two of the irksome kind during my long-distance ride from South Florida to Canada. They taught me an important lesson. I was pedaling along a secondary road bypass around Jesup, on the way to Odum, Georgia. I had left Route 301, the old interstate, at Jesup. When I finally arrived in Odum, I discovered it was a small town divided into two sections by railroad tracks and a handful of stores along the main street which parallel the tracks. But getting there by my route seemed impossible. As I turned down the intended road, which appeared to be the most direct route, a sign loomed ahead. DETOUR — BRIDGE OUT — LOCAL TRAFFIC ONLY. An orange arrow, outlined in black, indicated where I was supposed to head to circumvent the temporary obstacle, a bridge under construction. I couldn't tell from the road ahead, beyond the detour sign, just how far away the bridge was located, so I hailed a passing motorist.

"Bout two mile down the road, beyond that rise ahead," he replied, pointing a finger through his pickup's windshield to where the pavement lifted over the hill and dropped out of sight

43

among some trees.

"And I guess the town's on the other side of the river?" I asked, my map in hand.

"Yep."

"Well, how far around is the detour?"

"Let's see, 'bout two mile down thataway to the next paved road, then hang a left and go another mile, cross the old bridge, then two mile back to town."

"Five miles then?"

"Yep. Want a ride? You can throw your bike in the back."

"Uh, no, no, I guess not," I answered hesitantly, silently debating if detours counted in a bike trek, or whether one could just subtract the total from the detour and shove accepting a detouring ride back far enough in one's mind so it wouldn't nag after the trip was completed. After all I wasn't responsible for the detour. However, I thanked the man who had offered me a free ride and waved him along his way.

Reluctant to add five miles to the trip if I didn't really have to, I edged around the barricade and rode down the empty "LOCAL TRAFFIC ONLY" road toward a house in the distance, on top of that rise my informant had indicated. An electrician's truck was parked just off the road, alongside a breezeway from the house to its garage. He was on a ladder, installing a lighting fixture. A woman who seemed in charge of the household stood below him, watching his installation. They both turned as I rode up.

"I was just wondering if I could get across the bridge ahead, the one under construction up there," I asked.

The woman said nothing. The electrician, expressionless, said, "Didn't you see the sign BRIDGE OUT?"

"Well, yes," I answered lamely, "but I thought maybe with just a bike and all, there might be a way."

"Sign says the bridge's out," he stated, turning back to the dangling fixture. "That's all I know about it." The woman shrugged her shoulders and said nothing. I thanked them, turned away and rode to the top of the rise. In the distance, I could see assorted pieces of equipment, some yellow trucks and another barricade stretching across the road where it apparently moved down to the distant, invisible stream itself. I gazed disconsolately, shrugged as the woman had done, turned and pedalled reluctantly back, retracing my path past the house and on back to the barricaded corner. I turned onto the detouring route to pedal the five miles out of my way to Odum, muttering to myself about detours being real downers.

As I finally entered the village, I passed what appeared to be the only cafe in Odum. The man who had offered me a ride was just leaving the restaurant to climb back into his pickup's cab.

"Hey, there," he hailed, "just talked to some of the bridge crew having lunch. They would have let you walk your bike across on the barge they're working from to repair the bridge. It's wide enough to carry the beams and stuff they need, but not for cars or trucks."

"Bummer," I called back, shaking my head and spitting out a silent, one-syllable expletive. Had I ridden up to the bridge, I would have discovered for myself that my situation did not fit the typical one for which the road warnings were designed. I could have saved myself time and effort if I had merely investigated the problem from my own perspective, not that of other travelers along that particular road.

The next detour I encountered several days later reinforced my determination to look at situations from my own point of reference, and not that of society's in general, be it that of a lone cycling traveler along vehicular roadways or someone moving along life's twisting, unpredictable pathways in general.

That second detour sign was another of the "LOCAL TRAFFIC ONLY" variety. I surely did not qualify as local traffic, but I decided to ride up and check it out. Sure enough, there was room for me along the temporary single lane open to traffic coming and going through the area under repair, but not for the tractor trailer behemoths sharing the highways and most of the byways in our well-traveled nation. I had saved myself miles of needless pedaling by taking a gamble. I could have obeyed the sign and simply detoured around the area. From my road map, it appeared to be a few miles longer the detouring way, but my gamble to pedal along the "LOCAL TRAFFIC ONLY" section paid off.

As I rolled along that day and the ones to follow, detouring preoccupied me. How many times in life do we meekly follow the arrows, skirting our problems or those of others close to us because it's the easiest way out, because it's what most others would do, because not following the arrows would be impractical, out of the norm, and would seem "odd" to others traveling the same paths?

Dwell for a few moments upon some of the wellworn paths medical care providers have insisted upon historically, from

THE GOODALL House historical plaque was one of hundreds passed on my upcountry trip. The two-story Goodall House is the only dwelling standing today in the area. Never underestimate the power of prayer — nor its duration!

blood-letting, a common practice 200 years ago, to today's highly skilled wielding of scalpels to create detours around internal, problem-producing pathways instead of looking carefully for other possible ways to clear up the congestion of traffic flowing through the myriad highways and byways of our bodies and minds.

I'm not for a moment suggesting anyone ignore the detour signs of life. But I'm certainly going to remember that morning when I wasted valuable time and energy simply because I didn't bother to discover just WHAT was necessary to be detoured, and why the signs were erected in the first place. Now, *voluntary* detours are another matter entirely.

One great advantage of traveling alone, self-contained, on a bike is that you have only yourself to please. That is, you can stop anywhere if you feel so inclined and linger as long as you like without worrying about another's desire to get on with the trip. If you're able to just "follow your bliss," to quote Joseph Campbell, the late, great mythologist and teacher, you quickly lose that self-imposed burden of worrying about what a companion might consider as too frivolous. Consider the morning I crossed the Altamaha River on State Route 121 in southeastern Georgia and discovered the "GET BUTT NAKED" bridge.

I had no idea it was so labeled when I first pedaled across it. If fact, anyone who merely drives or walks across that level, short concrete span without bothering to look underneath it, would never realize why that written command exists. I discovered the reason, merely by chance.

I was nine days out of West Palm Beach, and beginning to really feel at one with my bicycle-seated view of the world. Birdsong had accompanied me from dawn 'til dusk up through Florida and Georgia. Most recognizable and most persistently present along my nine-state route were the varied cries of the cardinal. The male's vivid red plumage, coupled with the female's more subdued, but just as perky appearance, have delighted bird-watchers as perhaps no other bird. Their willingness to come to backyard feeders from Maine to Florida and across the entire

Midwest has gladdened the hearts of bird lovers since backyards were hewn from the forest primeval. The cardinal's song, so distinct as I spun silently along the roads, seemed to assure me that all was well. I had spotted both males and females almost every day traveling north. Their calls seemed always within earshot.

Most common was the consonant-chopped chirp of alarm, but that morning, a cardinal was declaring its territorial rights with its signature call, three identically pitched short, upward swoops of single redbird syllable "wheet, wheet, wheet" then the lyrical, slowly falling long note "chewoo, chewoo, chewoo" streaming down from higher pitched, more quickly paced piping. The call was so arresting among the midmorning murmurs of the rural countryside that I felt compelled to stop and see if I could spot its source. I decided to wheel my bike into some tall grass covering a slope descending from the road level toward the end of the bridge.

As I settled quietly down beside *Sir Walter* in the grass, its fragrance engulfing me, I glanced back under the bridge. There was the lazy stream, tea-colored, flowing slowly, reflecting sunshine. It was all but invisible from the road above.

As I turned again and gazed upward, hoping to glimpse the so-far invisible cardinals, I could hear the water running below. Some streams do murmur, you know. One of my life's dreams always has been to have a hideaway cabin beside a murmuring brook. That compelling sound forced me to turn to the stream again and, as I looked back up the waters to locate the reason for the murmuring, I spotted the girders which supported the bridge's span from below. There, along the center of the nearest girder, in bold, spray-painted black letters was the phrase, "GET BUTT NAKED."

I almost laughed out loud at its audacity. I always had thought the middle word was "buck," and my mind wandered from the hidden redbirds to a possible reason for that bold message. Of course, it must have referred to the water beneath the bridge, but I could see no evidence of anything wider than that shallow, rock-strewn stream. Could there be a swimming hole

"GET BUTT NAKED" sign under a bridge in north Georgia.

nearby?

Then, the clear, crisp call of a cardinal caught my ear and I turned downstream, away from the bridge. I couldn't spot the bird through the foliage, but there was sunshine glinting from something through the underbrush. I slid noiselessly down the slope from where *Sir Walter* lolled, and peered through the bushes. The cardinal's call had stopped, but something else attracted me. There it lay, downstream — a dark pool with a dam of fallen trees and brush at its far side.

As I picked my way through the dense underbrush, I could see a path coming from the other end of the bridge, down alongside it, across the stream I had heard murmuring. The path turned toward the pool. Sand had accumulated on that far side. That bank was covered with bare footprints. Some led up to the huge log that had created the dam. Apparently, one could jump or dive from that log into the pool below. As I weaved in and around the tree roots and river debris toward the other side of the pool, I glanced back under the bridge again. There, clustered below the girder with the commanding phrase, were spray-painted hearts with initials inside, and other initials linked by pluses, "Ike + Jenny," and an anonymous confession, "I love Marylou." Farther on, on the abutment supporting the girder, was the single word, "YES!"

As I picked my way across the stream to the other side,

toward the pool, I heard a car rumble across the bridge above me. A canopy of densely leafed tree limbs hid the pool from the sight of anyone crossing the bridge. The sun had barely penetrated the pool's leafy bower. As I hunkered down at the dark water's edge, the rush of memories of swimming holes past swept away my thoughts of locating the cardinal's call.

I recalled Dam Number Four on the Des Plaines River north of Chicago's far northwest side. In our early teens, we'd have our moms pack a lunch and we'd head out the highway northwest of Chicago, through Park Ridge, toward Curtiss Airport, seven miles away. That small, grass-runwayed place now is sprawling O'Hare Airport, one of the busiest skyway terminals in the U.S. On our way, we'd stop at Dam Number Four.

In the springtime, the always muddy waters behind the dam would rise high enough to allow us to go swimming. We never told our folks if we decided to take a dip because we had been warned not to trust that murky place. "There may be raw sewage in there," my mother would admonish. We never lingered long. The water was too cold, but there were always the "I dare you" taunts, and finally, committed as we'd strip to our skivvies and run for it, "Last one in is a rotten egg!"

As I began to remove my shoes and socks at the edge of this southern pool, just to see how cold the amber water was, I recalled another pool, much colder and clearer. It was part of a tumbling trout stream in central Wisconsin near the tiny village of Saxville. It really babbled! How surprised I had been that late spring morning as my father and I fly-fished along its banks. We both were sweating in the late-morning sunshine. "How about a dip in that pool up ahead," my dad suggested.

"But Pop," I exclaimed, "we forgot our suits."

"Aw, we'll duck around behind that big boulder there, away from the road. Let's make it quick." Open-mouthed, I watched him start to loosen his belt and bend down to kick off his shoes. Silently we both shed our clothes, back to back, then turned and leaped, feet first, yelling, into the rapidly flowing water. Both of us were good swimmers, and had to stroke hard to stay up behind that boulder. I can still feel the shock of that cold water. We swam hard for the bank where we had left our things, slipping over the rocks on the bottom as we struggled ashore. I can remember turning my back to him as I dried off as best I could and buttoned up my shirt and pants. We had never done this before together. We never did thereafter. My father simply was not the type. It was wonderful.

"Now, don't go telling your mother about this," Dad warned. "She'll think we do it every time we go fishing."

"Nosiree," I answered. I don't recall ever stealing a refreshing moment that way with my own son. Life's not over yet.

I noticed the tea-colored water in that north Georgia stream was tepid compared to that Wisconsin river. And its hue recalled the Grassy River near St. Lawrence University in Canton, way upstate in New York, which also was bordered, in part, by pine trees. The tannic acid from their needles also dyed that frigid water that amber shade. In Georgia, where tree farms abound, it's not surprising to find the waters so dark.

Yes, I thought about those wriggly creatures who also enjoy such verdant habitats as I inched my way out into the pool. But consider the world from their perspective. If one lets them know one's going to share a little of their world by moving slowly and splashing a bit to warn them one's visiting, they'd take the hint. If you were a small snake, certainly you wouldn't deliberately take on some strange being which towered above you, would you? Okay, some do, but why is it that so many humans deny themselves life's simple pleasures by imagining the very worst that could befall them? In our media-soaked world, we all know that stories about tragedies sell newspapers and improve TV ratings. They satisfy our morbid curiosity. If we're curious about natural phenomena, such as swimming holes which seem to have been tinted with iodine, even when those waters are cool and beckoning, we're considered foolhardy to test them. For me, this life is too short not to seize the day. So I stripped and waded in.

Ah, those Puritan forebears of ours did a job, didn't they? To swim nude in a public place was a sin then, and it remains so now in most parts of the "civilized" world. Maybe that's why I relished it so, wallowing in its wilderness of delights. So suppose I was trespassing. So a sexagenarian cyclist frolics nude in a hidden pool for a few brief moments as he discovers its wonders. So arrest him for leaping off that log at the deep end of the pool into its murky depths, butt naked.

There was an anxious moment.

As I dried myself off with my T-shirt, I noticed the grass parting ever so slightly about four feet from the water's edge. At that moment, I recalled a marvelous line or two from an Emily Dickinson poem. "He likes a Bogey Acre," she wrote, "A floor too cool for corn..." Well, here came what she was describing, almost at my feet. I must admit that I reacted the same way she did, "But never met this fellow/Attended or alone/ Without a tighter breathing/ and Zero at the Bone—-"

My involuntary shiver at the sight of the blacksnake passed in an instant. Perhaps two feet long, he glided by and slipped into the water at its weedy edge, hunting for lunch, self-contained. I, too, decided to glide away and leave this sylvan glen to find my own repast. I was happy that I hadn't met that "narrow fellow" at eye level as we both were swimming, but I was invading his territory. He hadn't intruded upon mine. How pleased I was that the elusive cardinal that morning in north Georgia had whistled its siren call. Such gifts Mother Nature provides — birdsong in the morning and starshine at night.

SKINNY DIPPING after following the advice of the sign.

CHAPTER SIX

DRIVE-BY SHOOTERS, FAMOUS POET, AND FANS

**If a man be gracious and courteous to strangers,
it shows he is a citizen of the world.**

— Francis Bacon

It's neither the distances you covered, nor the scenery you've enjoyed; it's the people you meet. They make the deepest impressions.

Most cyclists I've met who have undertaken extensive tours, in both books and in person, seem to echo this sentiment. But why is this such a universal feeling among those of us who bike longer distances?

I can only draw from my own solo experience. But those who tour cross-country in groups with "sag wagons" carrying their gear say about the same thing. Yes, they agree, most memorable are the folks you meet, most of whom seem to go out of their way to be kind. However, cyclists on commercially organized rides invariably include those new friends who ride with them as much as they do the folks whom they meet along the way. That's only natural. I'm sure backpacking hikers feel the same kinship with those who walk and/or climb with them. For those who ride or tramp on foot in pairs or in groups, it may have to do with varying degrees of shared hardship.

Acquiring aches and pains, sweat and strains together seems to be a catalyst for camaraderie. Any "Doughboy" of the World War I era, "G.I. Joe" of the World War II era or "Grunt" of Vietnam will understand. Shared pain increases shared pleasures after the misery has subsided. But what about the solo cyclist?

I discovered that the greatest antidote for fatigue or depression was meeting someone on the road. Of the dozens and dozens of people I talked with or waved at along the way, only one was outright surly. She was a gray-haired, passing motorist driving a battered pickup truck along State Route 321 in South Carolina. I was hugging the outboard edge of the right-hand white line as usual as she approached. For what seemed to me some unknown reason, she slowed, leaned over toward me and shouted, "Just get off the damned road!" Never swerved to threaten me, or stopped to berate me, just yelled in passing. Perhaps she had suffered some emotional upset that had nothing to do with me, or maybe it was the T-shirt I was wearing. I'll never know for certain, but my apparel could have triggered her outburst.

Shortly after she had hurled her epithet, a carload of youngsters passed by. One stuck his head out the right, rear window as they were passing and yelled, "Cool T-shirt, man!" I was wearing a faded, green West Palm Beach Bicycle Club shirt. On the front was a circular shape of words identifying the club. On the back was a prominent black arrow pointing upward. Underneath were the letters "BIKE LANE."

Perhaps the grumpy pickup driver was irked because those two words seemed impertinent. Who knows? I hadn't moved from the narrow shoulder of the road. The vast majority of the back roads I used had narrow or no shoulders. However, that latter "cool T-shirt" comment buoyed me for several miles. Cyclists do have a perfectly legal right to ride on roads. However, all wise pedalers use discretion and ride as far to the right as possible. We NEVER should ride

BIKE CLUB shirt that attracted the only shouted complaint directed at me during the entire trip. A passing female motorist shouted, "Just get off the damned road!"

against the traffic although I saw youngsters and adults alike break this cardinal rule whenever I rode through a town of any size.

Most strangers who met me on the road were kind as well as curious, particularly in the rural South, with only one notable exception. Almost everyone I met and stopped long enough to chat with was interested in how far I had come and how far I was going. Perhaps my almost-white hair prompted their ready warmth.

Of course, bicycles themselves usually are symbols of congeniality. Bicycles warm hearts as well as brows. They conjure fond memories. They were our first vehicles to truly help us sever the ties of apron strings. Our two-wheeled magic carpets gave us our first taste of real freedom from authority. We savored our adventures along the mysterious highways and byways of human travel beyond our front gates or stoops. Also, a bicycle's lack of internally combusted power and serenity of motion fosters a non-threatening feeling of cordiality for strangers whom we encounter. Here we are. At least wave "Hello" if you can't come along with us.

Only one other time did I encounter outright human hostility along the way from South Florida to Canada. I was riding on Route 321 and had crossed the Savannah River which separates Georgia from the southernmost of the Carolinas. I was determined to get to Columbia, South Carolina's state capital, sometime during that Memorial Day weekend to meet James Dickey, a prize-winning poet and author. I had been thinking about Dickey ever since I

A CLOUDY DAY on the Savannah River bridge just entering South Carolina.

55

crossed into South Carolina on that bright morning in late May. I had just finished eating lunch in Fairfax, a rural hamlet, and was musing over questions I would put to Dickey as I pedaled along Route 321. I had no idea that I was about to become the victim of a drive-by shooting.

I never heard the car approach. As the elderly brown sedan crawled by on silent tires, I glanced over toward it just as the barrel of a gun was aimed at me out of the rolled-down window.

After the first shock of seeing the gun and being hit at the same time, I flushed with anger. After I wrote down the license plate number, I wiped off the side of my head and began to calm down. The kids were out of sight around a bend in the road. What could I do even if I had called the local sheriff? It may have been a drive-by shooting, but being hit by a squirt gun hardly ranks as a particularly vicious crime. I did keep a sharp eye out ahead and in my rearview mirror for that nondescript brown sedan approaching again as I continued down the road, but my momentary tormentors never returned. Perhaps it was just as well. It would have been one against six. As the miles piled up, stretching away from the scene of the "crime," I forgot about the incident as another small town loomed ahead. My next encounter with a carload of teen-agers was of an entirely different nature.

It was Reidsville on Route 321. As the afternoon was lengthening I pedaled past the one-block business district. Plenty of parking spaces were in front of the stores. As I moved past the last of the small business buildings, a white Baptist church and on toward the other end of the hamlet, a carload of young people, both male and female, passed by. One pretty young girl, maybe 16 or so, waved at me from a rear window. The driver, a young man, glanced over, too, and pointed at me. I waved back, following my primary rule of the road — Always Be Friendly.

After the encounter with the squirt gun-toting carload of teen-agers, I realized that motorists, particularly in groups, could lead to something unexpected, so I mentally noted the make and model of the vehicle. However, it already had turned a corner and was out of sight around another corner by the time I had reached the intersection of the next street. Just moments later, I heard the squeal of tires behind me, the sound they make as they careen around a corner. I moved over, closer to the curb, checked my rearview mirror and stopped to look over my shoulder. There came along the same car as before with the same cargo of cavorting passengers. I decided to stay on the street side of the curb as they approached.

Instead of slowing down, they speeded up to what must have been the speed limit of that small town, and turned ever so slightly in my direction. I didn't feel threatened, but couldn't help but recall the drive-by shooting. Just as they passed by, everyone in the car was laughing and waving at me. No stealth here. The driver flipped what appeared at first to be a large, white balloon out of his window. The balloon flew up, lifted by the eddies of the car's wake, and wafted over the street toward me. It settled to the grass at the roadside. I was taken by the youngsters' lighthearted welcome to their community. Now, wasn't that friendly of them, I thought to myself. I walked over to the balloon, and realized that it was not at all what it seemed. With a wry grin, I bent down to pick it up, realizing why all the boys and girls in the car had been so animated as the driver launched his object of what I took to be a gesture of friendship. Well, it could be construed as that, in an oblique way.

The kids had decided to inflate a condom, tie its open end and toss it to me like a flower of welcome. My, how times have changed since I rode with fellow student friends through a college town, large or small! I mused for many a mile after that upon our AIDS-aware society in all its dimensions. Can you readers of the pre-baby boomers generation imagine scurrying around among your assorted pockets and/or purses during a spin around town to see who has a spare, er, "rubber" to toss to an ancient touring cyclist passing through the neighborhood? It never would have happened co-educationally when I was their age. Not that I had led a particularly sheltered life, growing up in Chicago, but there have been dramatic shifts in social mores from pre-World War II to the post-Desert Storm era. Oh, we adolescent males may have carried the things in our wallets all right, carried them for so long the elastic ring would be imprinted in our leather wallets. But they usually were secret symbols of bravado, not to be tossed out of car windows, inflated, no less, in mixed company at that.

Another symbol of changing times and/or the proximity of late adolescents, usually males, was the approaching rhythmic thump, thump, thump of a four-wheeled vehicle's stereo sound system. Dear to the ears of loud music-loving motorists of a certain age are "dual voice coils," "tweeters" and "polypropylene woofers." Woofers are circular gatherers and conveyors of "low-end response" (low frequency sound waves). These loudest of speakers can vary in circumferences less than eight inches up to eighteen inches. Now, "subwoofers" are the amplifiers of choice for those who enjoy the feel of sound as well as its lyrical patterns.

Those invasive, nondirectional waves delivering the insistent beat, probably propelled by laser beam from a whirling CD, could be heard pulsing from a pickup, sometimes even before the vehicle drove into view. I recall a particular night along a north Georgia back road when apprehension crept into my tiny tent like a sub-arctic breeze as I heard that ominous beat.

I had waited too long to locate a suitable camping site as I pedaled north-by-northwest up Route 301. Dusk was falling, and all around were recently plowed fields. It was peanut-growing country, and in some sections, planting was the preoccupation. I turned off 301 onto a gravel road, and geared down. The gravel thinned to sand as the private lane narrowed. Up over a distant rise must have been farm buildings. I tried to keep moving along, looking for a way to get across or through a barbed wire fence surrounding an empty field, freshly furrowed. A line of thick bushes next to the field, but inside the fence, offered a protected spot. If I could find an opening through the fence, perhaps I could walk the bike along the unplowed edge and find a level piece of ground between the bushes and the field to pitch my tent.

I had trudged, wheeling *Sir Walter* along the deepening tire ruts, for perhaps an eighth-mile when an iron-gated entrance into the roadside field on my left loomed up in the falling light. Just as I had loosened a strand of wire securing the gate to a corner fence post, and was lugging the bike through it, I heard the now-familiar boom, boom, boom of a mobile stereo system in the distance, back toward 301. It seemed to be coming down the gravel road. I slipped the gate back into place and dragged the loaded bike into the gloom of the bushes inside the fence. Crouching low over the bright orange covers of my saddlebags, I flattened myself out over the rear tire. The thumping of the bass tones of the music grew louder. The vehicle's tires crackled through the gravel beyond the trees and fence.

If the driver looked over, he or she would be certain to see me sprawled out there. Why hadn't I just stood in the road by the gate and waved at the truck, or tried to stop it to find out who owned the field? I knew why. It was that muffled, gut-stirring beat from the stereo system. Age's wariness of youth's strange noises. Does the beat of distant tom-toms cause pulses of alarm, stopping overland travelers in their tracks? This was no gossipy "island telegraph" that Jimmy Buffet sings about. This was darker, deeper, penetrating, mysterious. And it was headed my way.

I swept off my helmet, ducked down, cocking one eye sideways as the truck passed. Its windows were shut against the dust, their darkened panes hiding whoever might be peering at me. Strange how those low frequencies projected out through the steel panels, but the high notes were so muffled they were the mere crests of the thumping waves of sound below. No melody. No lyrics. No music. Just that flat, dark beat. The truck never slowed. As I lay there, eyes riveted to the stern wake its tires stirred up, the pickup's headlights flicked on. The sun had dropped down below the horizon. The pickup's taillights seemed like the devil's own eyes disappearing in the dust.

A few yards down along the edge of the field I could see a grassy strip large enough on which to pitch my tent. I dragged the bike down to it, still hunched over, the booming beat fading in the distance. Ah, the comforting cover of darkness. As soon as the light faded, I began to unstrap the tent and fly, relaxing, then realized that I wasn't at all sure of precisely where to pitch the tent. I stomped around the tall grass, tossing away broken limbs from the bushes, bending to dislodge rocks, clearing a small space as best I could by the Braille method. I was thankful that I had not accidentally plunged a hand into a fire ant's nest. The ground was hard, but tolerable. I was by now familiar enough with my gear to find sleeping bag, water bottles, flashlight, air mattress and other essentials in the dark. No lighting a fire tonight. I was a trespasser, homeless. I had just settled in when I heard that thump, thump, thump of the truck's stereo again. Or maybe it was another young maverick coming back down the road, just looking for trouble. There must be houses up the road over that next small rise. Perhaps the owner of the field I had stolen into was on his way back to run me off. I dragged *Sir Walter* farther under the bushes beside the tent and crouched inside. Headlights cleared the top of the rise, carrying along the gut-contracting beat. Strange how it pierced the darkness, void of any melody, only the tightening tempo.

It was the same pickup, black, one-way windows rolled up against the swirling dust, heading back toward Route 301. The truck never slowed as it swept by. Only the pulsing grew, peaked as the pickup passed, then died away in the dark until all was tranquil again. I vowed to break camp before daylight, head away from the forbidden land of the penetrating percussiveness. If it returned during the night, I didn't hear its "low frequency response."

I was careful to gather up all traces of my trespassing as the silent, thin pre-dawn light arose. By the

HIDING IN tall grass gives a camper a cozy, secure feeling.

time the sun broke the horizon, I was well on my way up Route 252, a paved county road running parallel to the busier state road. I hadn't paused long enough to fire up my one-burner stove, heat some instant oatmeal and top it off with some coffee. I was looking for somewhere where I could wash up, have breakfast, and shake the tensions of the night before. Hiding out behind hedge rows had left me uneasy. Being an overnight trespasser, as benign a lawbreaking as it was, was unsettling. I guess I should have gone right up to some farmhouse and asked permission to camp out in a front or back yard, or planned more carefully to be in range of a town with a motel come nightfall, but I hadn't and wasn't, so the hedge row night, complete with plenty of disturbing "low frequency responses" was added to the trip's notes. I'd try not to let it happen again. Encountering the booming of young adults' mobile stereo systems would be inevitable, but I could decide to sleep in more congenial surroundings, not slip surreptitiously under cover of darkness into the edge of a peanut field.

All of the apprehensions of the previous night were wiped away the next morning by the cordial welcome I received as I happened upon a true "general" store, the Ponderosa in White Oak, Georgia. It was located on Route 252 at a crossroads deep in the piney woodlands west of New Brunswick. The store's name didn't seem to fit the image of any of those towering trees of northern California. In fact, it seemed like any other rural crossroads store except that it could hardly be called a "convenience" store in the late 20th century sense. It lacked the packaged, plastic look of a place where only rapid turnover of merchandise was foremost in the minds of its owners. No, Ponderosa had a consumer-weathered patina that only several decades of daily dropping by can produce, where swapping stories was just as important as selling soap.

I could see through the screen door that the Ponderosa was open for business. It was 8:15 a.m. The front door was swung back inside. As I stepped across the unpainted boards of the porch to the threshold, I glanced up at the wall behind the staple grocery items shelves where canned goods dwindled off into auto parts, sets of tires, rakes and farm equipment. There hung on the back wall of the store was the largest mounted boar's head I had ever seen. Why, it was the only wild boar's head I had ever seen, mounted or otherwise. Its fierce tusks thrust out over the peas and tomato labels below, staring down my roving eye for ready-to-eat food.

I had been on the road since before dawn and was anxious to sit down to a breakfast. I hadn't taken time to stop along the blacktop to even fix myself a cup of instant cereal and coffee, but as I entered, and I was hungry, that huge boar's head startled me into other conversational avenues.

"Wow!" I uttered, mouth gaping. "Is that a pig?" I had noticed from the corner of my eye as I walked past the screen door an elderly black man with thinning grey hair, perched on a stool behind the cash register. He seemed to be working on a ledger, totaling up receipts, but had looked up from his figuring as I came in.

"Well, it's a HE-pig. Yes suh. My boy, Barry, surprised him one morning 'bout 20 years ago in our corn field. He had been tracking a deer, but that boar's rootin' had frightened them away. Barry and that boar were both surprised to see each other."

He had eased off the high stool and took two steps around the counter, as though he had risen from an easy chair to welcome a guest into his living room. "Barry got him right behind a shoulder as he lifted his head and turned to run. Dropped before he

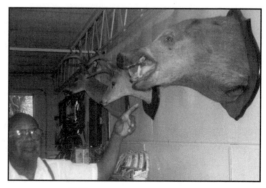

THIS MOUNTED boar's head in Mr. Reed's general store, Ponderosa, in rural eastern Georgia reminds him of his son Barry's confrontation with the 600-pound beast in a nearby cornfield more than two decades earlier.

took three steps."

"Gosh, I've never seen a mounted boar's head before," I stammered. "What did it weigh?"

"We figured about six hundred pounds. Butchered it right there in the field where it fell. Took two men, with them tusks as handles, just to tote the head out to the road." He walked toward the wall where the boar's head hung, beyond two mounted six-point deer's heads. I asked him if I could take a picture of him pointing to the boar's head. "Yessir," he replied, "but it's too bad Barry ain't here. He's the one who shot him."

I glanced behind him toward a far corner of the room. A door opened into another room where I could see the end of a bar and a corner of a pool table and some tables and chairs. "Bet you had a heck of a barbeque," I said.

"Yeah, the word got around pretty quick," the older man chuckled.

"Makes me more hungry, just thinking about it," I answered. "Anywhere around here I could get some breakfast?"

His face sobered slightly as he replied. "If it was the week-end, we serves sandwiches and such, but during the week most folks are working so we shut down the grill. You on that bike out there?"

"Yes, I'm headed up north."

"Where you from?"

"West Palm Beach, Florida."

"You ride that thing all the way?" His eyebrows lifted, eyes widening.

"Yep. I'm headed for Canada. Camp out most nights."

"Well, I'll be dogged," he said, voice dying. He walked stiffly to the door and looked at *Sir Walter*, shaking his head. "I'm 74," he said. "How old are you?"

"Sixty-eight."

"Well, I'm goin' strong, still. Seems you are, too. And you ain't had no breakfast yet?"

"Well, no..."

"Tell you what, just go over there to that card table set up there with the dried dog food display on it, over there by the TV. Here's a chair. Set right there. I'll see what I can find out back. Donahue's coming on right after the news."

"Hey, if you only serve on weekends, that's all right."

"Just set and relax. It'll only take a few minutes." And he disappeared through the door to what had looked like the weekend recreational area. I heard a heavy door open and close, like that on a walk-in cooler, then the subtle sizzle a frying pan makes. Then, the unmistakable odor of bacon curling, shrinking.

Not ten minutes later he came back with a plate piled high with grits, two fried eggs, and a thick slice of ham AND bacon slices, three of them. "Here's some vittles to hold ya," he said softly, a quiet smile accompanying the feast. "Your toast and coffee's acomin," he murmured over his shoulder as he dropped a paper napkin beside it and shuffled back through the store to what must have been the kitchen area to bring the rest of it. After he set the steaming cup on the table, he extended his hand, "My name's Reed, Leroy. What's yours?"

"Bostwick, Frank. I really appreciate..."

"Just eat," he interrupted. "I own the place. I can do what I want." As he moved slowly across the worn linoleum to where he had been perched behind the cash register on the counter top, he stopped to look at *Sir Walter* through the screen door.

"From West Palm Beach," he muttered, shaking his head. "My, my," and went back to his figuring.

I made quick work of all that had been set before me. Then, I set the empty cup on the scraped-clean plate, gathered up the napkin, knife, fork and spoon and stood up.

"Just leave it all right there," Mr. Reed said.

"What do I owe you?"

"Oh, let's make it two dollars."

I walked over to the counter to pay him. I would have gladly paid three times that much. "How come this place is called Ponderosa?" I asked.

"Why, I named it that. You know, the old TV program with Hoss and the rest of 'em. Had kind of a nice ring to it. Sounded better'n just 'Reed's Store,' don't you know?"

We chatted for a few minutes. Mr. Reed had started up his store shortly after World War II with his mustering-out pay. Built it himself. Had been running it since 1947 with his wife, Peggy. They have two sons, Barry and Shane. "Kept us out of the fields and the pulp mills," he explained.

I shook his hand again before I left. I wondered if he had been white and I black, that he would have bothered to stop figuring in his account book that weekday morning long enough to fix a total stranger breakfast. I hoped so. I think I would have named the store "The Boar's Head" or maybe "Stranger's Rest."

As I drew closer to Columbia, South Carolina, I began to notice the lift and fall of the terrain around me. The capital of that first southern state to secede from the Union, way back in 1861 after Abe Lincoln was elected President, was at the southeastern end of the Piedmont Plateau. Columbia was declared the state's capital in 1786 in the very center of the state for political reasons. The "upcountry" farmers, self-sufficient from the vast plantations along the coast, wanted equal representation with the powerful landholders in the more populated coastal areas, with their shipping headquarters to the world, the mighty port of Charleston nestled in its spacious, protected bay.

I would eventually skirt around the highest of the mountains in the Blue Ridge chain as I headed north into North Carolina, then across the very easternmost tip of Tennessee and on into Virginia and later, Kentucky. For the moment, however, I was preoccupied with meeting James Dickey. He had lived in Columbia for more than 20 years.

Major poets are not lionized in North America as they are, for example, in Russia, but Dickey has won major literary awards for his poetry and is widely recognized in the academic world for his critical essays as well. Few members of the general reading public would recognize his poetic works, but movie goers of the 1970s would certainly recall a film adapted from his best known work of fiction, *Deliverance*. Burt Reynolds starred in it as the most dedicated amateur outdoorsman among four urban sportsmen who meet their match on a canoe trip down a raging river in Georgia. Murder and other forms of malevolent violence abound in the film. Dickey made a cameo appearance as a backwoods sheriff. The movie made him more money than any poetry or teaching assignments ever had up to that time.

When I decided to ride north to visit my daughter, Cindy, in Port Huron, Michigan, I had two reasons for choosing to challenge myself with the Appalachian Mountains rather than ride up the flatter Atlantic seaboard, then turn west, say, between Washington and Philadelphia where the terrain was less mountainous. One reason was to experience real mountain riding, the other was to meet James Dickey. Major newspapers and other publications around the literate world noted with due respect his literary contributions following his death on January 19, 1997. *The New York Times* ran a half-page obituary.

For me, Margaria Fichtner, the *Miami Herald* book editor, captured his essence best: "When Georgia-born James Dickey died last Sunday two weeks shy of his 74th birthday, the world of what he called "liter-a-tour" lost not only one of its best poets, but also one of its most monumental characters, a swaggering storyteller defined by war, water, winds, and woods and driven by a fierce, unquenchable passion for the power of words to stir and redeem the soul."

I first heard him speak in 1963 at Western Michigan University in Kalamazoo near the very beginning of my college teaching career. He had left the advertising business in the 1950s to become a poet. Dickey had won coveted fellowships, major poetry awards both here and in Europe, and later became the only Consultant in Poetry to the Library of Congress to have served for two consecutive terms. At the time of his death, he was the Carolina Professor and Poet-in-Residence at the University of South Carolina. Besides publishing three novels, Dickey has 235 poems in print.

The America Literature text in use today at Palm Beach Community College where I teach describes Dickey as "everybody's notion of the muscular poet." The textbook's editors were referring to his passion for the "worlds of physicality, animals and nature." I had made a point of meeting Dickey in person in November, 1992 as he was autographing his latest novel, *To The White Sea,* during the Miami Book Fair. I told him I would be riding my bicycle through Columbia that following spring, and could I drop in just to say "Hello" as I was passing through?

"Why, I guess so," he replied in that luxurious southern accent. "You might call first to make sure Ah'm home. My numbah's in the book." I did.

He had lived in his relatively modest single-level ranchstyle brick house on Lelia Court in Columbia for more than 25 years. The house is clustered with others around a small lake in the heart of a thickly settled neighborhood of upscale homes.

Dickey at 70 appeared more rumpled than remarkable as he invited me into his home in Columbia toward the end of that Memorial Day afternoon. He was taller than I, above six feet, blond, dressed in a dark, faded T-shirt and a nondescript pair of pants, sandals on his bare feet. He gestured me inside.

"Want a beer, a soda or somethin?" he asked in his marvelous (to these Yankee ears) southern drawl as he waved me through the front door. It was a warm afternoon. I shook my head, apologizing for calling late the day before to set up the appointment on a holiday. I had phoned just as soon as I had located a motel room nearest his home in Columbia.

"Naw, I hadn't planned on driving any Memorial Day race cars. It's okay. Wife's around here somewhere. With my daughter, I guess. Maybe I'll get her to make us some spaghetti. It's almost suppertime." I assured him that wasn't necessary, just a few moments of his time was all I needed, and perhaps he'd read a poem or two from his works? I had toted a small tape recorder with me on the bike for just that purpose. I also had located and purchased a copy of his most recent book, *The Whole Motion— Collected Poems, 1945-1992,* in a nearby bookstore the day before and had devoured as much as time allowed in my motel room.

We walked through his wonderfully cluttered home. It

seemed full of bookcase-lined walls. Seven guitars and lots of archery paraphernalia were scattered around the family room. A grand piano, its top covered with framed photos of family members, dominated the living room. Dickey led me by the kitchen and onto a back porch, then down to a wooden bench on his dock. It jutted into what had been a lake, but had been drained temporarily for some unknown "municipal" reason, he explained, but he assured me it would be filled again.

"You say you teach American lit?" he asked as we settled onto the bench. I nodded. "Well, what's the first line of Stephen Crane's *The Open Boat?*"

"Why, uh, 'None of them knew the color of the sky.'"

"That's good. What about..." and he rattled off the first line of a Hemingway short story, something about two men sitting at a bar. I stumbled on it, flustered. He waved his hand. "Oh, that's okay," he grinned. "You did just fine with Crane."

Apparently I had passed the test. I wish I had turned on the tape recorder right then instead of much later as he read "In a Mountain Tent" for me. I wanted my lit students to hear it. We both liked the feel of tents around us in the woods, I discovered. Dickey, a gifted raconteur, told me about his two grown sons, Christopher and Kevin, his first wife, Maxine, and her death, his second wife, Deborah, a former student, and their 13-year-old daughter, Bronwen, his adventures on the set of *Deliverance*, his working with Burt Reynolds, his love for bow-hunting, his poetry.

I asked about his famous poem, "Falling." I had first read it more than a decade before in *The New Yorker*. It was the centerpiece of the February 11, 1967 issue. "Falling" just might have been the longest poem (175 lines) ever to have appeared in that mass-circulation magazine, Dickey stated, obviously pleased. "I know one thing for damn sure," he grinned, "they paid me more for it than any other poem I ever sold, before or since." I couldn't quite work up the nerve to ask him how much.

Dickey had noticed the news story of a flight attendant who had fallen to her death from an airliner. He began his tour-de-force with this stylized news quote: "A 20-year-old stewardess fell...to her death tonight when...she was swept through an emergency door that suddenly sprang open...The body...was found...three hours after the accident." — *The New York Times*

"Yes, I was quite excited about that one," he said, trying to keep from smiling too broadly." It did create quite a bit of attention. I wasn't sure when it would appear in print, but as I was boarding a plane from someplace I was lecturing — I forget where now — somebody said it had just appeared in the *New Yorker.*

"Well, the first thing I did after I got settled in my seat and buckled up was to see if they had a *New Yorker* to read. They did, but when I thumbed through it, I couldn't find the poem. The pages it had appeared on were cut out. Now, that's censorship!" he laughed. "Guess the airline didn't want to upset the passengers on that flight."

He talked and I listened. The sun had fallen almost without my noticing. He suggested we go inside to see "where the women are." We discovered they had gone out, so he insisted we go to a nearby restaurant to eat. From the greeting he received as we entered I realized he must have frequented it often. He asked for the table before the decorative fireplace, requested that its indestructible fire (a gas flame) be lit and ordered drinks. They knew what he preferred — martinis. I ordered scotch. When our drinks were served and we had ordered our meals, he raised his glass and stated, "You know what Jack London called this stuff?" I shook my head. "White logic!" he said, with a wicked wink, and took a generous sip. We both knew that famous writer of immortal tales of the Far North had died an alcoholic.

It was almost midnight before we returned to his home. He picked up one of seven guitars, propped haphazardly along one wall of his cluttered study off the living room and played one part of the famous "Dueling Banjos" from *Deliverance.* I have it on tape. My fantasy right then was wishing I could have picked up one of the other instruments nearby and played the way the musician with the answering banjo did in a memorable scene from the film. Of course, Dickey's late-night rendition didn't match the virtuoso performance by the two rustic banjo pickers featured in *Deliverance*, but I was enthralled.

Before I left, I asked him to sign his collected works. He wrote "To Frank — at the beginning — from James Dickey." His graciousness was the epitome of Southern hospitality.

One particular Dickey poem, "Vessels," came to mind as I heard of his death on President Clinton's second inauguration day. It began, "When the sound of forest leaves is like the sleep-talk / Of half brothers." I mused about our brief encounter on my cycling way upcountry. During those few hours together, we had shared our love of the out-of-doors, of the cozy feeling inside tents in the rain, of our vastly different, but equally appreciated lusts for life.

I left early the next morning for North Carolina, but not before pedaling to the main post office in Columbia to mail home a cardboard carton full of things I had decided to get rid of to lighten my load — extra bike shoes, long pants, scraps of the "safety orange" material, Lycra bike pants, extra spoke wrench, long screwdriver, used maps. Thoreau's words rang again in my head, "Simplify, simplify."

Still another example of the friendliness of Southern folk was to happen that evening. As I settled into my booth at a roadside restaurant 60 miles north of Columbia after a full day's ride on the open highway, a gray-haired woman with a small boy in tow stopped by on their way to where the

BIG GAME Check Station not only sells hunting and fishing licenses, but also checks game for legal size, weight and gender. Usual game are deer, turkey, raccoon and pheasant. Live game are not required to check in!

restaurant's hostess had beckoned them to sit.

"Excuse me," inquired the woman, "but were you riding along this road south of Columbia two days ago?"

"That's right," I answered. "Did you pass me?"

"Yes, I couldn't help but notice your orange bags and that pennant flying behind you. Where are you headed?" I told her.

"Canada! My, you have a long trip ahead of you. Where did you start from?"

When I answered West Palm Beach in Florida, she just had to ask how old I was. When I replied, "68," she gasped. "Why that's *my* age. You certainly are in great shape."

I thanked her and we chatted until her grandson began tugging at her to go to their table. I had picked the restaurant because it was one of those all-you-can-eat buffet places, so they left before I had finished my second helping and dessert. As I approached the hostess to pay my bill — by then she had taken her other station at the cash register — she raised her hand, "You don't owe us anything," she explained. "That lady you were talking with paid your bill."

"But I don't even know her name," I stammered, hoping the hostess might know who she was so that I could write to thank her.

"She's a stranger to me, too. Just chalk it up to Southern hospitality," the hostess/cashier smiled. I did.

One more total stranger extended a helping hand as I pedaled my way from South to North Carolina. Even though he was in the bicycle repair business, he refused payment after working for more than an hour on *Sir Walter's* braking system.

I had arrived in Gastonia, North Carolina, on Route 321, 16 miles west of Charlotte, about 9:30 a.m. After a night of tenting, I had noticed my left brake lever needed adjusting with a long-shanked screwdriver I didn't have in my kit of tools. The terrain was more hilly than on the previous day, and I used my brakes much more frequently than before. They needed adjusting.

I discovered that Cycling and Fitness, an attractive store on East Franklin Avenue, didn't open until 10 a.m. so I took the

STATE SIGN history lesson — North Carolina state line sign also reminds us it was the first state colonized by English settlers (1585-87) and the first to "vote readiness for independence, April 12, 1776."

Below: DRYING OUT while waiting for the bicycle store to open in Gastonia, North Carolina.

occasion to spread out all my gear in front of the store to dry in the morning sun. This was a daily excuse to stop in mid-morning all along my route. I'd stretch and nibble on a snack while my tent and attendant gear dried out. Whenever I broke camp at daybreak, both the tent and the fly were dripping with dew. That's what gives the Smokies and surrounding mountains their characteristic haze, plenty of early morning condensation.

Shortly before ten, a young man who introduced himself as Tim Baily opened the door of the bike shop. He seemed really interested in all my adventures so far, and started right in to check out the brake lever. He and his partner, Allen White, not only adjusted the brake levers, but removed the brake cables which ran from the handlebars to the brake shoes on the wheel rims to lubricate them. They also rewrapped my handlebars.

"What do I owe you?" I asked.

They shook their heads and refused to accept anything for their services. "We really didn't do much," Tim smiled. "You didn't need any parts, just an adjustment. Enjoyed talking with you." Just another example of Southern hospitality.

CHAPTER SEVEN

ON THE ROAD TO DAMASCUS

**Your armed struggles for profit
Have left collars of waste upon
My shore, currents of debris upon my breast.**

—Maya Angelou
On the Pulse of Morning

A paramount joy on my upcountry bike tour was the natural beauty that surrounded me much of the time. My greatest sorrow was what I found crowding out that beauty — litter, debris, waste, pollution. That is why a municipal campground in Mountain City, Tennessee always will have a place in my heart. The town is located along Interstate 421 at the northeastern tip of the Pioneer State, in the foothills of the Iron Mountain range. The community may not be litter-free, but its municipal campgrounds simply enthralled me that early June day. It was there that I became acutely aware of just how precious what is natural around us can be.

I had arrived in Mountain City at sundown after a relatively strenuous ride from Blowing Rock, North Carolina down through Boone, then over backroads across the state line into Tennessee. Blowing Rock had been the trip's high point geographically, 5,900 feet. But the lowest point for me, physically and psychologically. The area attracts mountain terrain lovers in the spring, summer and fall seasons and is a thriving ski resort in the wintertime. But I was struggling as passing cars and trucks kept me pinned to the white line on the road's edge for the last 20 miles of Route 321 up to Blowing Rock from another resort community, Patterson. The pavement had narrowed to two lanes. As the terrain grew more mountainous, the road's shoulders seemed

THIS NARROW-SHOULDERED road with a possible downhill tumble to the golf course below was conquered near Blowing Rock, North Carolina.

simply to shrug away, allowing me scant room to escape an errant vehicle coming too close for comfort. I had dropped to my lowest climbing gears, but it wasn't enough. As the dusk deepened, I walked the bike the last mile to a motel just south of Blowing Rock's village limits.

I stumbled in exhaustion through the front door of my assigned room after registering for the night, my quads still burning from the climb. Facing me across the room was its back door. What was a back door doing in a motel room? I opened it and limped onto an expansive back veranda which stretched the length of the building. Apparently every room had a back door which opened onto it. There, beyond and below me, was the Blue Ridge Mountain range. It stretched northeast far into the gloom of the gathering night. The dense forest hundreds of feet below masked the headlights from cars coming and going on the touring motorist's delight, the Blue Ridge Parkway, five miles north of this man-made mountainside perch.

My gloom melted away as I gazed across the magnificent

MY HARDEST day ends near Blowing Rock, North Carolina where I walked the bike the last two miles to a mountaintop motel. I'm getting the hang of the self-timer.

green expanse. It wasn't Longfellow's forest primeval, but his "murmuring pines and hemlocks" offered up a balm inexpressibly soothing. I'd call Kate. We'd spend a second honeymoon right here if I discovered the road ahead of me to be as difficult as the one immediately behind me. I'd come this far on these 68-year-old legs. Maybe this was far enough. I'd sleep on it, then decide. A hot bath never felt better than the one that night.

The next day's gain far exceeded the previous day's pain. The road leveled out as it passed the area's biggest tourist draw. Blowing Rock was a tiny, almost inaccessible mountaintop village in the 1920s, but in recent years the area had bloomed into a resort developer's dream.

The "Rock" was named for the curious way breezes from the valley below would swoop up under an ancient outcropping jutting from the very peak of the mountain I had climbed the night before. Link that natural phenomenon with the legend of a lovestruck Cherokee Indian chief leaping from the rock to his death below because his intended's father wouldn't allow her to marry him. Her desperate prayer as the despondent brave was falling to his doom caused the winds to lift him back up to the rock on which she stood, wringing her supplicant hands. Her father was impressed and granted the young couple permission to marry.

Tourists flock to the well-manicured location. They pay $4.00 each to visit the site, peer through coin-grabbing telescopes at nearby peaks, nibble on overpriced sandwiches, and browse in the well-stocked souvenir shop which they must pass as they walk from the legendary outcropping high above the green forests back to the parking lot.

I paid the four bucks. It was worth it to see the peaks below me, especially now that I had been told the roads ran downhill from there to Boone, my next stop.

I was truly delighted to discover that the roads did seem all downhill from Blowing Rock to Boone. I passed under the Blue Ridge Parkway just north of Blowing Rock. It traverses through North Carolina for 241 miles. This first designated national scenic highway is ideally accommodating to bicyclists, I was told. No commercial vehicles were allowed, and the speed limit was 45 miles per hour. The parkway connects the Shenandoah and Great Smoky Mountains national parks. Its elevation averages 3,000 feet, with several designated recreational sites along the way.

Just before entering Boone, the town with a distinctive western flavor, I passed the "Horn in the West," an amphitheater where, in the summer tourist season, a state-sponsored dramatization of Daniel Boone's life story is presented. It prominently features his leading local settlers in battle against the British and Indian forces. Boone's family emigrated from Pennsylvania to North Carolina in the 1750s. I wondered what his forebears, peace-loving English Quakers, would have thought about modern day dramas featuring his military exploits. Unfortunately, I didn't delay my trip long enough to enjoy the local open air show. I also wanted to poke around the campus of the Appalachian State University in Boone, but of first priority was to improve my ability to negotiate those Appalachian mountains ahead. I was bent on locating a bike shop. I really needed a lower gearing in my bike's drivetrain in anticipation of the rugged terrain ahead.

Three high-spirited young men of Boone Bike & Touring, Bill Pressly, Dirk Brown and Michael Baldwin, relieved my hill-climbing anxiety by providing an invaluable technological lift. I knew that I needed a different combination of gears on my rear wheel than those with which I had begun the tour. Both genial

Joseph McColly, owner of the Bicyclery in West Palm Beach, and Tim Bailey of Cycling & Fitness in Gastonia were sure the original gears on the bike were sufficient to get me through the mountains. I took their word for it, but discovered my legs, at least 35 years older than theirs, simply weren't giving me the pedal power I required to make it up those blue-ridged hills.

But the Boone boys had the answer. They installed a six-freewheel "cluster" of gears on my rear wheel hub. The largest had 32 cogs. Freewheels spin "free" if the cyclist stops pedaling and coasts.

As a hill became steeper, I would downshift to the smallest of the three chain rings on the crank set (where the pedals are attached). That smallest chain ring has 28 cogs. Then, I'd shift to the new 32-cog freewheel on the rear hub. I was now in what is called a "granny gear," a sexist label from an earlier era. It simply allows for more leverage in each push of the pedals. It is easier to pedal up an incline. That bigger 32-cog freewheel on the rear hub, linked with the smallest of the crankset hubs, gave me the power I needed. Actually, when I think of that gear, I always conjure not an elderly matron but a male character on the old comedy TV show "Laugh-in." Others my age will remember that disreputable old man in a battered hat and raincoat riding the tiny

AFTER-LUNCH SIESTA. Just find a level spot, spread your ground cloth and snooze. These were wonderful, without shoes of course!

tricycle. Remember how he would pedal furiously, all hunched over on that trike, then tip over sideways? That TV descendant of the classic slapstick banana peel routine helped keep me in relatively good spirits as I struggled up those inclines through the southern edges of the Appalachians.

I would be "spinning" as hard as I could push the pedals, refusing to dismount until the last possible moment, when the bike was barely moving. Sometimes, if the shoulder of the road was bordered by high grass, a relative rarity in that rocky terrain, I'd ease the bike down into the verdant cushion and sprawl out, spread-eagled beside *Sir Walter's* steel frame. Although puffing, I'd chuckle as I'd recall that old man in the raincoat, toppling over on his tiny trike. Visual images of past pleasures diminish present pain. But then almost invariably as I lay there, reality would intrude. I'd see or feel marks of modern man — his discards: cans, candy wrappers, crud. Litter abounds wherever one loiters along roadsides in this grand but oft-times gritty land of ours.

A day later, as the terrain became more cyclist-friendly, I didn't have as frequent eye-to-ick contact with debris. Not that it wasn't there; I just didn't collapse as much amid it. State Route 421 sloped gently downhill from North Carolina's border to Mountain City. I could spin along in comparative ease, no longer having to stop so often to catch a much-needed breath.

Arriving in Mountain City at dusk, I immediately began to scout for a proper place to pitch my pup tent. I found it toward the northern edge of the community, stretched out along the highway in Johnson County. The sign beckoned "Welcome Center Campgrounds." I turned off the highway and pedaled across Furnace Creek. The crystal-clear stream separated the bustle of the town from the natural rising tranquility to the west. The road into the campgrounds wound around a hillside up to the Welcome Center itself, perhaps a hundred feet above the entrance off the highway.

Co-sponsored by the local Chamber of Commerce and the local historical society, a simulated log cabin had been built along the crest of a mini-plateau overlooking Furnace Creek and the highway beyond. Its wide front porch offered two picnic tables and a magnificent view, but the center was closed for the day.

Tacked to the front door was a diagram indicating the sites for RVs and their hookup facilities. Several other sites beyond the RV sites were for tent campers. They were farther up on the slope overlooking the stream. The campgrounds were empty. I decided to play it safe and check with the local gendarmes before pitching my lightweight tent. I had noticed on the posted diagram of sites that the charge for camping was $5.00.

One uniformed officer was leaving for the day, and another was arriving for the night shift as I entered the community's police station, less than a mile away. Neither one knew precisely to whom the envelope containing my five-dollar bill should be addressed, so I merely handed it over to the man behind the desk and asked if there was anything I needed to fill out.

"Nope," smiled the officer. "We know where you are. I'll swing around later to see how you're doing. It's usually pretty quiet around here." He did, and it was.

That night I slept as soundly as I ever had in my pup tent. I liked the feel of the place. Rising more than 1,100 feet behind me was the beginning of the Iron Mountain range, serenely majestic in its leafy robe of trees, vines and underbrush. If I had been a backpacker, I would have headed northwest for about 20 miles the next morning on 421, which blended with Routes 34 and 91 to reach the Holston Mountain range. Along its ridges ran the famed Appalachian National Scenic Trail. But I was planning to leave Route 421 for the portion of Route 91 which followed the Tennessee Laurel Creek flowing through the Cherokee National Forest. I was bound for Damascus, Virginia, having passed through the northeastern most tip of Tennessee.

During all of that cool, moist early June night, the rising mountain greenery surrounding Mountain City helped muffle the rumble of an occasional passing truck along the highway below. I could still hear that proverbial "murmuring" of Furnace Creek between me and the four-laned asphalt ribbon. The stream's name undoubtedly was linked to the mountain chain.

MY GEAR aired out after restful night in Mountain City, Tennessee. Note my pitched tent appearing as a small white dot in the distant background.

Historically it must have played a role in the smelting and processing of iron ore. Cottonwood trees, clumped along the far side of the creek, blotted out the one-storied municipal buildings, quick food eateries and other commercial stands along Route 421. They also helped muffle the sporadic whine of tires on the highway below me.

All was shrouded in mist the next morning, from the mountain's crown to the brook below. A pair of cardinals, with irritated chirps of controlled alarm, complained about my presence in their habitat. I lugged my tent, which was dripping with dew, up to the front porch of the Welcome Center. As the rising morning sun burned away the mist, I emptied the contents of my saddlebags onto a picnic table to air them and cooked myself a leisurely breakfast of hot instant cereal. I had developed a preference for packets of Quick Quaker Oats (with cinnamon!) because they were lightweight, easy to prepare — just add hot water — and nutritious.

A light breeze from the south began to waft through the Welcome Center's veranda. Good! I would be heading north. Cyclists always pay attention to which way the wind is blowing. I sighed happily, brewed a cup of instant coffee (it also came in lightweight packets), and decided to read a few pages from Thoreau's *Walden*. Although a touring cyclist's major concern is the weight of gear carried, my pocket-sized edition, a few ounces, was worth its extra weight to me. Thoreau's words of woodsy wisdom were welcome companions.

One phrase caught my eye as I sipped my coffee, "Not till we are lost, in other words, not till we have lost the world, do we begin to find ourselves, and realize where we are and the infinite extent of our relations."

This particular sentence spoke loudly to me. I was not physically lost, but I was beginning to realize an urgency I had not experienced so acutely before. Humankind had become lost to the awareness of its intended role in nature.

I rose and zigzagged my way down the path marked in the steep hill from the Welcome Center to the burbling stream below. A mallard and his mate swam leisurely upstream as the mist

HOW GREEN was that valley in the northeastern tip of Tennessee. This scene was spectacular in its natural colors.

began to lift. They glanced at me crouched on shore, but paid no mind. They seemed to sense my inner calm as I contemplated the "infinite extent of our relations."

Just beyond my feet, below the surface of the rippling water, nestled among the slippery slabs of shale, was a lone can of beer, still ensnared in its plastic, six-ringed holder. No other cans were in sight, either unopened or empty. Perhaps the person who left it to cool had disposed of them properly in one of the receptacles placed around the campgrounds.

But the lone can and its six-pack ring stuck in my mind as I began to pedal my way north by northwest on the road to Damascus along Route 91.

On the road to Damascus. That phrase re-echoed as thoughts do when one's spinning along a less-traveled road, hour after hour. I recalled a Sunday school teacher through the mists of more than half a century, telling us about Saul on his way to Damascus in Biblical times. She held us spellbound with the dramatic tale of a heavenly light that flashed down on Saul, blinding him, and the solemn words he heard, asking him why he was persecuting their heavenly speaker, asking why he, too, had not seen the light.

She explained how Saul then changed his name to Paul and became the greatest of all the early Christian preachers.

These childhood Sunday school memories welled up as I rode along the road to Damascus. I was following the course of the Furnace Creek whose ancient streambed had laid the first pathway through these Appalachian foothills toward Virginia, long, long before our nation had been divided up into states. My thoughts had mingled with the early morning vision of that crystal stream in the mist (and the lone can of beer with its constricting ring). All the whispering greenery I was passing suggested I play the old "What if...?" game.

What if Paul had not received only those riveting words from on high, "Why do you persecute me?" which changed his life instantly? What if, in the solitude of his blindness and then, as his sight returned, in the months within which he recuperated on some Arabian oasis, what if, in a still, small voice, a divine whispering also seized him?

"Look about you, here, as you rest and recover from your revelation. Notice how our mother, Earth, provides for us. Be sure, as you pass along the Good News, to urge your fellow men and women to have a real reverence for not only Me and my Father, but also deep respect for the source from which you ultimately receive your physical sustenance."

You may be muttering, "But isn't this all covered in Genesis, when humans were given "dominion" over all the earth and its creatures?" I know, but we're still playing "What if?"

Forget that egocentric "dominion." What if, in some heavenly way, shape, or manner, the idea of the divine right of the earth to provide for all of us had been conveyed to Paul, the man destined to become the known world's greatest spokesman for Christianity? What if that "divine right" would never be interpreted in the same way as it later was misconstrued as the "divine

IRONIC JUXTAPOSITION in Kentucky where a sign stating "TREES GROW JOBS" is placed next to one stating, "ADOPT A HIGHWAY. LITTER CONTROL NEXT TWO MILES." Tree farms provide wood to be turned into pulp for paper products but, of course, the pulp mills are a source of pollution, and considerable paper ends up as litter. We face difficult priorities/balancing decisions.

right" of kings and queens to have the power of life and death over their subjects? Would it have changed the way we treat the earth?

I am not suggesting we treat the earth as an object of personified worship. But why can't we treat her with simple reverence?

The stewards of our continent before 17th century European humankind immigrated to it were Native American Indians. Their spiritual beliefs instilled in them a true bond with their brother: the buffalo, for example, whom they thanked each time they slew one for its gift to ease their hunger and their need for clothing and shelter.

It was a natural way of life for the Indian tribes whose ghosts moved within these very mountains I was pedaling through. Their settlements didn't wipe out their means of sustenance the way our cities wipe out nearby streams and lakes, polluting them so ruthlessly that they're rendered unfit for drinking or swimming.

What if, even when our population did begin to soar — it doubled in the U.S. between 1870 and 1890 — fervent voices rose from all the lecterns, pulpits and altars throughout our land: "Let us praise God on high, and revere Mother Earth as the vessel of all divine gifts through which we receive the Ultimate Gift, life."

If that fervor continued into the late 20th century, reminding kids in school to recycle, why, collecting cans, bottles and various plastic shapes and depositing them in the proper receptacles might be considered a holy act by us true believers.

See how upcountry bike riding tends to make your mind not only wander, but wonder, too? What exciting flights of mid-morning fancy one can take while spinning along "the roads less traveled by." It happened to me on the road to Damascus, Virginia.

Chapter Eight
"The Friendliest Town on the Trail"

As the Spanish proverb says, "He, who would bring home the wealth of the Indies, must carry the wealth of the Indies with him," so it is in traveling, a man must carry knowledge with him if he would bring home knowledge.

—Boswell
Life of Johnson

Shallow memory sometimes accompanies deep thoughts. Did you ever ponder a problem while traveling along a highway or byway but, when you arrive at a destination, can't recall clearly the scenes you passed while getting there?

It was that way for me about recalling the small village of Laurel Bloomery along Route 91 in Tennessee just a few miles south of its border with Virginia. I discovered after my upcountry trip that while I was musing that bright June 10th morning about humankind's environmental sins against Mother Earth, I had cycled right through the small town with the flowery name without remembering any details of my surroundings. All I remember is thinking how Aaron Copland's symphony "Appalachian Spring," harmonized (forgive the pun) perfectly with that village's name.

Well, Laurel Bloomery must be special in the spring for the nearby profusion of blossoms, but I had arrived three weeks too late for that. However, I later discovered that its nearby inhabitants had produced something much more enduring than springtime flower blossoms. More than 65 of them had created distinctive stoneware in a small factory near there from 1964 to 1992. Stoneware. You know, very durable plates, platters, cups, saucers, bowls, mugs, jugs and other tableware. If a teacup, for example, rings when you flick it with a fingernail, chances are it's stoneware.

Nancy Patterson Lamb of Damascus had co-founded the company Iron Mountain Stoneware in 1964. Its products have been recognized internationally for their fine quality. Each piece of stoneware was formed, decorated, and glazed by hand under Mrs. Lamb's tutelage. She first became fascinated with clay after World War II as an art student at the Los Angeles Art Center College of Design. While traveling abroad for seven years, she designed ceramic art in Denmark, Finland, the Middle East, India and Asia before settling in Tennessee.

I regret not realizing that a factory producing artistic stoneware reflecting the talents of mountain people was right on my route. For more than 28 years, Iron Mountain Stoneware shaped "the earth into lasting beauty of form and color," according to a brochure produced during that time. Another source, Ronald M. Fisher's book for the National Geographic Society, *The Appalachian Trail*, explains how Mrs. Lamb, then Ms. Patterson, and Albert Mock founded the factory in cooperation with the U.S. Department of Labor. More than 400 unemployed people in that economically depressed area applied for the first 15 jobs available. The owners, wrote author Fisher, decided upon the factory site in Laurel Bloomery because they were eager to "escape the turmoil and high costs of urban America, [and] partly to take advantage of the traditional handwork interest and aptitude of the Southern mountaineers."

Mrs. Lamb, who continues to create decorative tiles in her studio, Good Earth, behind her home in nearby Damascus, explained by phone why I wouldn't have been able to take a tour of the factory as I pedaled through Laurel Bloomery in 1994. It had been closed. "We just couldn't keep going anymore because of rising costs," she explained. "You see, we 'high-fired' the kilns with propane gas. This 'high firing' fuses the clay body materials into a very dense material impervious to absorption." Mrs. Lamb pointed out that "high temperature ware is like a piece of granite, harder than steel."

No lead was ever used in the glazing process for Iron

Mountain Stoneware, but it's been used in firing clay at lower temperatures since glazes were first developed to make earthenware non-porous or for decorative effects, Mrs. Lamb explained. The problem with using lead in glazes, even though it melts at much lower temperatures, is that "it can leach out from the dish into the food consumed. NOT a good idea," she warns. As the cost of propane spiraled upward, so did insurance rates and other costs of producing the high quality stoneware. Finally, overhead and in-kiln costs forced the factory to close. Wages had increased too. "It was very hard to shut down. Our folks in the factory always had been like family. They were truly splendid," Mrs. Lamb said.

She had designed 26 different patterns which reflected the natural beauty in that mountainous area of northeastern Tennessee and southwestern Virginia. Consider just two pattern names — "Martha's Flowers" and "Just Apples." They reflect not only the personalized charm of individual artists, but the flowing natural beauty and abundance of the region. Every piece was hand painted. Iron Mountain Stoneware became widely distributed. To coin a phrase from Copland's description of his lyrical "Appalachian Spring," Mrs. Lamb's superb stoneware also is "in the American vernacular."

In 1996, she explained for me that some of the stoneware she designed already have become collectors' items. "Why, two sets of my dishes sold for $2,500 each at auction in Abington (the county seat) recently. They sold for $400 each when they were first produced." Tammy Blevins, manager of the Iron Mountain retail store in Laurel Bloomery, still had a few pieces produced by Mrs. Lamb's company left for sale as this was being written.

Had I passed through that village at the very northeastern most tip of Tennessee just three weeks earlier, I would have discovered the Trail Days Festival in Damascus in full bloom just seven miles away, across the state line in Virginia. That "Trail" is the famous national scenic hikers' mecca, the Appalachian Trail. Not only can a traveler arrive by car, truck, or bike, but through the years thousands of hikers have visited Damascus,

YOUNG "A.T." hikers rest and check maps in Damascus, Virginia where the town's main street is part of the Appalachian Trail.

too. They descend from the Trail along ridges of nearby mountains into the town. This backpacker's mostly wilderness pathway stretches for 2,100 miles from Georgia to Maine. Near Damascus, it follows the Holston Mountain Range, drops down to the town and passes through its main street, then up again into the surrounding mountains.

In 1985, Damascus village council members and other community leaders organized the festival to celebrate the town's growing reputation as being "the friendliest town on the Trail." Many knowledgeable thru-hikers, at least, who had experienced more than merely the Damascus area of the "AT" (as they call it) have tagged the town as "most friendly."

As I cycled into the village, I didn't realize that the Trail passes right down Laurel Avenue, the main street, and past stores, garages, and service stations. Hikers usually pause at C. J.'s Market or Cowboy's Minute-ette for a snack or at least to savor a soft drink. Some might head directly for the Post Office for a package they may have forwarded to themselves or to pick up mail forwarded to them.

Other thru-hikers might head for Mt. Rogers Outfitters. I dropped into that backpacker's paradise to buy some freeze-dried food. Just add water and heat. I also picked up a shirt-pocket-sized, waterproof notebook. I have a hunch the store owner's son, Jeff Patrick, prefers trout fishing to any other outdoor activity: "I can walk out of my store in any direction and be fishing within a few minutes. This is one of the 10 best places for trout in the U.S.," he remarked proudly. Three streams flow into town from different directions: The White Top, the Beaverdam and the Laurel Creek. We chatted about the wide variety of flies and fishing tackle he stocked, but I was more curious about bike riding in the area. Mountain bikes are "in" these days, especially in states with hilly terrain. Even in flat Florida, far more of the "fat tire" bikes are sold than standard touring bikes like my trusty *Sir Walter*. Jeff stocks plenty of mountain bikes for rent, and a few for sale. He explained a growing attraction is a bike shuttle service from Damascus up to Abington, the county seat 17 miles west by northwest. There, cyclists can ride along the former roadbed of "The Virginia Creeper" railroad line. It once ran from Abington into North Carolina as far as West Jefferson. Rails to Trails, an organization dear to the hearts of outdoorspersons everywhere, has been converting abandoned railroad tracks to hiking-biking trails across the nation for several years. The "Creeper" trail from Abington to Damascus, generally paralleling Whitetop Creek, continues for another 17 miles to the foot of Mt. Rogers, Virginia's highest mountain (5,729 feet).

Another entrepreneur in Damascus, Phoebe Cartwright, realized in 1991 that the rising interest in mountain biking might afford a business opportunity. She launched the Blue Blaze Bike and Shuttle Service in Damascus. Ms. Cartwright offered 25 bikes for rent by 1996, either by the day or half-day. Any cyclists with their own bikes can get a lift for $10 to the White Top launching site. Rental bikes go for $25 per day. Busiest times are from March to November. In fact, as of this first writing (1996), environmentally concerned authorities in western Virginia are considering limiting the number of cyclists per day using the Creeper Trail during the summer months to preserve the quality of the wilderness pathway in that area.

I have regretted not riding the 17 miles up to Abington from Damascus northwest on Route 58 before heading more directly toward my ultimate destination, Canada. Ms. Cartwright explained that Abington was the county seat, and historically as interesting as Damascus. The Blue Blaze Bike and Shuttle owner added that it was the oldest town in western Virginia, having been settled in 1776, more than 15 years before Damascus. The availability of natural resources for building materials there was more abundant and enduring than those near Damascus, then known as Mock's Mill. "They had the bricks, we had the lumber," she stated.

Those "bricks," of course, may have been made from some of the same clay deposits that attracted Mrs. Lamb back in the early 1960s. Her beloved Iron Mountain Stoneware factory may now be in the past, but Mrs. Lamb is very much in the present. She, too, is pre-occupied with bricks these days — bricks for a new project, The Friendship Path. Inspired by the continuing success of the Trail Days Festival, now in its 11th year, the internationally known ceramicist will design personalized bricks for anyone who contributes $50 to the continuing construction of the Friendship Path. Since April of 1996, more than 150 of these individualized bricks have been included in the ever-lengthening sidewalk. It is 64 inches wide and stretches for two-thirds of a village block along Laurel Avenue through the center of the Damascus business district. Phase One of the Path begins at the corner of Laurel Avenue and Shady Avenue. It stretched 135 feet by May, 1966. Eventually the Friendship Path will run down both sides of Damascus's main street.

This cooperative community project involves not only the village council but also the Virginia Department of Transportation, the Damascus Volunteer Fire department, and many individual citizens besides Mrs. Lamb. Two other Path

Committee members are Sandy Hart and Dave Patrick.

If you hanker to immortalize your name on a specially glazed brick to be laid into the Friendship Path (up to 60 letters are allowed) on a 7 5/8" x 3 5/8" paver, get an order application by writing to FRIENDSHIP PATH, c/o Good Earth, P.O. Box 340, Damascus, VA 24236. Nancy Lamb will work out a design and/or lettering to your specification.

Sixteen teams of world class racing cyclists zoomed through Damascus on Tuesday, May 7, 1966 during the seventh stage of Tour DuPont. The 112 riders were headed from Wytheville, Virginia to Bristol, Tennessee, 20 miles west-southwest of Damascus. They had begun on May 1st in Wilmington, Delaware. Lance Armstrong, star of the U.S. team, won that race.

Trail Days each spring brings back more than 1,000 folks who have hiked some part of the AT in the past. This "reunion" during the second weekend in May — it has even spread unofficially for a few days before and after that — coincides with what is hoped to be the most blossom-bursting time of the year.

Louise Fortune Hall, 85, a retired teacher and local historian, estimates at least another 1,000 visitors will join the AT hikers next May for Trail Days to enjoy the festivities. Arts and crafts of all kinds are displayed for sale then. "We really look forward to the Hikers' Parade and their Talent Night. There's a big barbeque, too. Why I couldn't get from my house across the main street last year, the crowds were so thick!" Mrs. Hall exclaims. She researched and co-wrote the town's history since its founding in 1793 up to 1950 with her daughter, Eleanor. Mrs. Hall and Marilou Hall Patterson have added the *History of Damascus, 1950-1978* since then.

If everyone is as friendly as Mrs. Lamb, Ms. Cartwright, Ms. Hall and young Jeff Patrick, the reputation of the town for being the friendliest on the Trail is secure.

I passed north by northwest through Damascus on Route 91 on June 10th. After a late lunch in the Trail Inn, I thought about detouring to pedal to the foothills of Mt. Rogers by turning east on Route 58 in the village. My copied section of the DeLorme topo map indicated it would have been another strenuous day's ride to get a good glimpse of Virginia's highest mountain. Judging from the tiny, winding, black-dotted line on the map marking the Appalachian Trail, backpackers get a closeup and personal look at the peak. I chose to keep on my riverside path along Route 91. Of course, those gray altitude lines on the topo map were pinched together by the Clinch Mountain range ahead on Route 80, too. Challenging mountain routes were all around me, but I had chosen the route as the most direct one through the range. By the end of that day I had reached Hayter's Gap. The steepest grades were just ahead, but it wasn't the grinding pace that was the most memorable there, it was a four-footed challenger who resented me even more than the mountain roads seemed to. His bared canines almost spoiled my next up-and-down day. I met him in the heart of the Clinch Mountain range. Judging by his nasty disposition, he certainly couldn't have come from the friendliest town on the Trail.

CHAPTER NINE

DOGS, DEER AND THE COURAGE OF TURTLES

He prayeth best who loveth best
All things both great and small:

— Samuel Taylor Coleridge

"What about dogs?" was a frequent question asked by other cyclists as I shared tales of my touring adventure from Florida to Canada. I have never heard of a cycling death-by-dog, but every bicycle enthusiast can come up with a favorite story about a close encounter of the canine kind. I had only one serious confrontation on my trip north. First, a preamble.

Dogs are man's best friend, right? Perhaps, unless the two-legged pal is riding a bicycle. There are many theories about why dogs chase bikes. One is that the spinning wheels seem an irresistible temptation. Maybe it's merely the excitement of flashing, circular motion. Could it be that the whirling spokes elicit some kind of centrifically induced magnetic aura undetected by mere human ears that draws sensitive dogs to chase spinning circumferences, inducing vocal protests? That could explain why my favorite childhood pet, Skippy, a Springer spaniel and excellent retriever, simply could not resist chasing after slow-moving cars passing by our suburban Chicago home. He would race headlong toward them, snarling at their spinning wheels. We bystanders, shouting at him to desist, were terrified that he would slip under a rear wheel and halt his frenetic attacks forever.

One morning, my father gave me instructions to gather as many tin cans as I could find. When I had collected half a bushel from garbage cans along the alley back of our home in Edison

Park, Dad told me to get into the back seat of our car, roll down the window and dump them on Skippy as we drove by the house. The determined dog never separated friend from foe in his frenzied habit. As he raced alongside, barking frantically, I dumped the cans. After one thunderstruck yelp, Skippy turned tail and disappeared around the side of our house. We found him cowering under our rear porch. He never chased another vehicle — car, truck or bike. There were times on my trek north when I longed for a basket of thunder-striking tin cans.

A second canine-vs.-vehicle theory is that dogs instinctively will chase bikes, cars or any other moving thing which invades what they consider their territories. This seems reasonable, but let us not ponder further. What did I do to protect myself? As little as possible. In fact, I rather looked forward to the canine encounters. I even tried to set up what professional photographers call a "shoot" when, as I rounded a corner in a small Georgia community, five dogs, all nondescript, but loud and lively, scooted out from under the wooden-floored porch of a general store. They seemed more like a welcoming committee than watchdogs because they bounded along the road's edge, rather than sweeping across the asphalt toward the bike. They yapped awhile, ears flopping, tails wagging, for about 20 feet, then turned back to the store. All of them headed back under the porch. I decided to try for a group action photo.

As unobtrusively as possible, I rode around the block where the general store was located, got my light, self-focusing 35-mm camera from its bag, held it at ready with one hand and steered with the other. Exactly tracing my previous path, I rode slowly by the store again. Not one of the hounds, large or small, moved. They lay, chins between paws, watching me pedal by. I even stopped and called to them. They didn't budge. One welcome was enough for each passing cyclist.

I have read about the odor of fear humans exude while being suddenly pursued by any threatening thing, and that animals instantly detect it. It may trigger hostility among some more aggressive canines. Consider horror story writer Stephen King's infamous Cujo, in the book by the same name. That crazed dog certainly would be a cyclist's nightmare. Fortunately, I never was cornered by a rabid, 200-pound Saint Bernard along the way from south Florida to Canada. Whether that body odor theory is fiction or fact, I try to appear as indifferent as possible to an aggressive bark or display of fangs. On the trip north, I did my best to control my musk. It seemed to work in all but that one encounter, that day on Clinch Mountain in Virginia.

I can't really bring myself to ward off a threatening animal by spraying it with Mace — I carried some along but never knew quite where I had packed it away — or throwing pepper in its face. In the first place, dogs have a way of appearing abruptly. My first impulse has been to keep on riding at my accustomed touring pace of about 12 mph rather than fumbling for a weapon. I did read somewhere of a cyclist who, in great haste, pressed the trigger atop a cylinder containing paralyzing liquid while aiming it at a barking dog, only to discover, belatedly, that the nozzle was pointed toward him instead of his alleged attacker. Only his forward momentum kept him from intercepting the full force of the powerful jet of fluid.

If the dog supposedly threatening me came too close on my upcountry trip, I would shout as forcefully as possible, "STAY!" Most times, it at least delayed the excited canine. If it continued to chase me, I sped up. However, occasionally this only seemed to stimulate the dog's efforts to snap at that moving knee or heel. I have tried to execute a well-placed kick at a snarling face, but the instability of the moment somehow always spoils my aim. Then, there's the problem of recovering as quickly as possible to get my foot back into the pedal strap to keep up my miles per hour. Usually, dogs will chase a bike only as far as the borders of the territory they feel duty-bound to defend.

Every time, I would get a little edgy about the potential threat of angry dogs on my trip north, I'd try to think of a funny story about dogs in general. After all, most of them chase anybody who comes along, regardless of the cyclist's er... — pedigree, so to speak. Consider the remarks that Noel Coward, that late, great British actor and playwright, made one day as he was walking along the seaside at Brighton with Laurence Olivier and his young son. As the threesome strolled along, the young boy pointed to two nearby dogs copulating and asked what was going on.

"It's like this, dear boy," explained Coward without hesitating a moment. "The one in the front is blind, and the other kind dog behind is pushing him."

If I wasn't in the mood for a bawdy guffaw, I'd recall a remark by another Britisher, Beatrice Campbell, whose wit and verve enabled her to create the role of Eliza Doolittle in George Bernard Shaw's *Pygmalion*, a famous play which inspired *My Fair Lady*.

Campbell was regaling admirers with a story about the time she tried to smuggle her Pekingese through Customs by tucking him inside the upper front of her cape. "Everything was going splendidly until my bosom barked," she explained.

One suggested maneuver: if you are threatened persistently by a barking dog, stop, dismount, and keep the bike between you and the dog until it realizes that you are merely a passing visitor intent upon leaving as rapidly as possible. The whirling wheels no longer are irresistibly exciting. The thrill of the chase has subsided. "No big deal," the dog mutters to itself, and you're out of there.

"Wait a minute," interrupted my cycling buddy, George B. recently. He lured me into this sport in the first place. During a recent weekend ride, we were discussing the fine points of discouraging aggressive dogs. "That tactic has a flaw," George explained. "I had two dogs chase me one day, one on each side. I wasn't about to dismount." His solution: Pick up the pace and hope for the best. It worked, and he escaped unscathed.

On two memorable occasions, I was unable to pick up my own pace because I was trapped in my own tent. Just past midnight on the 17th day of my tour, I lay curled up, sound asleep inside my pup tent. I had moteled it the night before in Winnsboro, South Carolina, catching up on my laundry and luxuriating in clean sheets on an innerspring mattress. On June 1st, after a relatively uneventful day of travel, I approached the outskirts of Clover, just south of the state line into North Carolina along Route 321. The sun was setting, and I was searching with increasing concern for a campsite. I had slept in open fields before, but they usually were in more rural areas. As the sun dipped out of sight, I pedaled by what seemed to be an abandoned house on the edge of a dense woods. Its front yard was high in weeds. Next door was a singlewide mobile home. Its porch light was on, but no cars were in the driveway. On the other side of the apparently abandoned home, lay the forest edge. I dismounted and wheeled *Sir Walter* around to the back yard of the empty, two-story house as quickly as possible. My plan was to pitch my tent out of sight behind a wood shed located behind the house. It blocked the view to the house trailer on the other side. I had eaten supper at a roadside cafe before sunset. All I had to do was to find a level spot, pitch the tent and crawl in, unobserved.

As I wheeled the bike through the uncut grass, I noticed that it had grown even taller in the backyard of the house. So much the better. I was in luck. I would be hidden from view, but in a relatively protected place. That is, off the main road and behind a house. As I pitched the tent, I noticed the faint outline of a narrow path which ran diagonally from where the trailer home was located in the next property past where I was located and on into the thick underbrush behind the shed. Just after midnight, I realized who kept that path faintly visible — at least one small dog.

I am a relatively light sleeper, even when I've been riding my bike 12 hours. I heard the startled "woof" shortly after midnight by the green-glowing hands of my wristwatch and raised my head toward the sound. There, in that narrow path was a small dog. It hesitated before it began to bark in earnest. I could not see what kind of dog it was, but the reflection of the porch light from the mobile home next door cast just enough light for me to make it out. Then, it started to yip in ever higher tones.

I lowered my head back down on the folded clothing I used as a pillow. The mosquito netting, of course, had been zipped up, but it would offer small protection if the dog wanted to scratch its way into the tent. The mutt's tenor yips allayed my fears of any immediate harm. I had only startled it in its nightly explorations. But its yelps were persistent and seemed so loud that the whole neighborhood (there were houses across the road from the mobile home) might be aroused. I lay immobile, mouthing a stream of curses that even surprised me. Would that damn dog ever stop?

Suddenly, the door of the mobile home opened. "Shut up you! Shut the _____ up!" the voice raged, and the small dog took off. It never came back. I never knew to whom it belonged. I must have awakened a dozen times, peeking at the illuminated dial of my watch. Just before dawn, I gathered up my dew-soaked gear and sneaked out of my abandoned backyard camp-site, praying that the yipper would not return. It didn't and I was out of there.

Six nights later, I was discovered by a dog, but this time, I was awakened by the almost silent sniffing of its nose, seeming-ly inches from my ear. Again, only the netting of my tent sepa-rated me from it. Earlier that day, I had been approaching my first serious mountain-climbing challenge since Blowing Rock. I had knocked on Mr. Robert Holmes' door in Hayter's Gap near Meadow View, Virginia — I had read his name on his mailbox — and received permission to camp in his spacious half-acre back yard. It featured a well-weeded vegetable garden. I inquired if he owned any dogs. He smiled and shook his head. "My wife likes cats." I heaved a sigh, and explained that I would be gone by first light. As I walked my bike around his house, two penned dogs owned by his neighbor next door barked for a few moments. One had that deep, lovely bay of a true hound. The other, out of sight inside a small farm outbuilding, was another yipper. He didn't see me, but yipped whenever the hound dog bayed.

Ole Yeller next door quieted right down as I settled inside for the night, and I heard no more from the tenor. Until later.

Again, shortly after midnight, I heard the sniffing sound near my ear. I lifted my head ever so slowly, and there, not three feet away, was another small dog. However, it must have seen the tent

98

in the half moonlight and had not realized anything alive was inside. It, too, woofed in surprise, but stood its ground and started to yip even more persistently than the one a few nights before had barked. Apparently, it had either been released to roam by its owner next door, or it had escaped its pen on its own after dark. Now it was barking. Loudly. Then, the hound joined in, but rather half-heartedly. It had seen me arrive, get permission and set up my tent. Its single, deep-throated "woof" was a token bark at best. I decided to remain silent, and lowered my head in resignation. Perhaps this would be the last time Mr. Holmes would be so gracious to a touring cyclist. I cursed the second yipper who had awakened me within a week. Finally, he, too, stopped before any porch lights winked on and angry humans protested. As I tip-toed past Mr. Holmes' house the next pre-dawn morning, I thanked him silently for his hospitality. The yipper was nowhere in sight.

However, that memorable Day After Damascus brought my bare knee to bared fang from Cujo's cousin just after I had conquered Clinch Mountain. The actual climbing time was relatively short, but I had used up almost all of my physical energy. I had shifted into the lowest gear possible. To keep my mind off the grind, I began counting the revolutions of my pedals per one-tenth of a mile on my odometer. They totalled 86, a proverbial snail's pace. Finally I cleared the crest. There was no magnificent view of other snow-capped ranges in the distance, the kinds on postcards the cross-country cyclists send back home as they pause beside a spring snow bank while crossing the Great Divide, or whatever. The Appalachians offer few spectacular views as one rides through them, but their leafy mountaintop woods are just as welcoming to a cyclist pausing to catch his breath.

Still gasping, I began to coast down the switchbacks on the other side. My quads burned as only sorely taxed muscles can. There were 23 zigs and zags through hairpin turns before I finally reached the leveling off into the valley below. My hands were beginning to cramp from gripping and releasing the brakes as I glided down, coasting all the way.

Just as I rounded the final curve, where the ground leveled enough to allow foundations for human habitats, a blur of canine fury appeared at my right knee. The dog's fur was long-haired, mottled gray. Of medium size, the attacker appeared to be a mixed breed, but its teeth seemed enormous because they were so close before I even realized they were there. Snarling never seemed so menacing before. Low and serious. The canine cursing before the ripping of flesh and muscle.

I spun my pedals frantically. To my dismay, I had forgotten to shift back up to a cruising gear from the lowest one needed to climb the steep grade. I had never pedaled so fast, but progressed so slowly. Just as I thought certain that the furious dog would succeed in sinking its teeth into my bare leg. I heard a voice behind us boom, "King! NO!" The dog dropped from sight. After I jiggled the gearshift into its proper position and the chain links clicked into their proper cogs, I glanced back. There, in front of his singlewide trailer home which had been invisible to me until I turned that last sharp curve, stood a tall, black-bearded mountaineer. He didn't wave. Neither did I. The dog stood at his side, panting.

When I was a safe distance away, out of their sight, I slowed and dismounted. The dog's saliva had not quite dried from the flesh of my right calf. I walked my bike until the trembling subsided.

As I traveled through the rest of western Virginia and on into eastern Kentucky, I kept a wary eye out for dogs, but no others displayed the sudden, unexpected ferocity of King. I would have renamed him, "Fang." Although dozens of other dogs offered up their obligatory yelps as I rode by their domains, or momentarily raced alongside the road's edge, they kept their distances.

Gradually, the terrain relaxed. It stretched out of the mountains and sprawled gently into the broad Ohio River Valley. I had realized why I had not avoided King's attack. Restricted visibility blocked my view of him. As I swung around that last curve, he, too, was startled. After all, it wasn't as if I were a loaded coal truck grinding down one of those mountain switchbacks in low gear, warning all ahead that something big and bulky was on the way. His master, whose authoritative roar had turned King in his tracks, apparently hadn't seen me coming either.

Within the next two days, after passing through eastern Kentucky and crossing the Ohio River, the great, fertile, flat farmlands of Ohio stretched ahead of me. I could see far ahead. Most of the farm dogs merely watched me pass as I cycled up the roads to Michigan. Forewarning of my passing tended to disarm them, and my momentary encounters with cranky canines subsided.

Only one other beast of any dimension was startled by my presence on the road north — an adolescent deer. As I journeyed through Georgia and South Carolina, birds and their songs seemed to set the dominant tones of nature. As I climbed through western North Carolina toward the Appalachians, my thoughts wandered to visual images of larger, landlocked wildlife. I knew that black bears rarely were seen outside of zoos, but I had read

THIS IS a dangerous highway because of the iron guard rail and no shoulder but the road offers a scenic view of part of the Daniel Boone National Forest waterway.

about the resurgence of deer populations where their food supply was plentiful. Stringent hunting laws were the keys to their survival. However, it wasn't until I passed through eastern Kentucky that I spotted the one and only larger animal to literally cross my path.

I was approaching Daniel Boone National Forest on State Road 519 on a warm June mid-afternoon when up ahead on the asphalt appeared an unsure-footed animal. At first glance, I thought it might have been a rangy mule coming down the center of the asphalt toward me, unaccompanied. Its ears seemed uncharacteristically large. I reached as quickly as possible into my front, right pannier pouch where I kept my lightweight binoculars. I stopped my bike and focused on the moving animal. No mule. It was a deer! From its wobbly gait, I sensed this could have been its initial encounter with a highway's hard surface. Its forelegs seemed to slip and slide as it trotted tentatively down the middle of the highway. I could hear its cloven hooves clatter. It almost lost its footing as it saw me and turned suddenly off the pavement and down the slight grade toward a fenced field on my left. No mule ever could have vaulted a fence in its path as that graceful creature did. I watched through the lenses for as long as I could see his white "flag" of a tail bobbing along through the field of grain toward the cover of pine woods beyond. How awkward the youngster had appeared on the highway at first sight, and how sure-footed it was on its own turf. Thousands of deer are killed by cars and trucks each year on our nation's highways. I rejoiced as this one made his way safely across one of man's treacherous black ribbons. Perhaps confronting a slower, quieter two-wheeled vehicle woul somehow increase its chances of avoiding inadvertent slaughter-by-car/truck in its civilization-bound future.

All cyclists along highways and byways are aware of "road kill." We who ride in groups on weekends in suburban or rural areas dodge the freshly bloated and/or finally flattened remains of small animals each time we venture forth. Passing motorists, encased, seem unaware of the indifferent carnage. I've even seen a T-shirted ad for the "Roadkill Cafe" on one burly trucker climbing out of his cab at a rest stop in South Carolina.

Besides the usual mangled dogs and cats, cyclists skirt around the flattened remains of possums, raccoons, squirrels, rabbits, mice, rats, birds, snakes, turtles — victims of velocity all. I realize this will continue for as long as animals attempt to cross busy highways. Tennyson's famous line, "Nature, red in tooth and claw," has merely extended to the nature of cars and drivers, too. Life is precarious, both inside and outside the vehicles that we drive. But while I toured those highways and byways less traveled by, I tried to assist at least one creature to cross safely — the courageous turtle.

There was a time when "courageous" was an unknown adjective for turtles in my adolescent vocabulary. Armed with a single-shot .22 caliber rifle as a youth on summer vacations on the edge of a central Wisconsin lake, I had destroyed, wantonly, most of the road-killed creatures listed above except dogs and cats long before I had a legal license to drive a car. Especially turtles. Was this latter-day, late middle-aged gesture a penance self-imposed for almost forgotten sins? Perhaps. And where did I get the idea that the lowly turtle is courageous? I recall the title essay in a remarkable book, *The Courage of Turtles*, by Edward Hoagland. I had never known that "turtles cough, burp, whistle, grunt and hiss, and produce social judgments." Those "social judgments" refer to the quick shoving of one turtle by another moments after both appear to be conversing silently, but with apparent amity. Hoagland never explains why in his otherwise informative, charming collection of animal stories.

Each time I'd spot a small turtle lumbering across a rural highway (Georgia turtles seemed most determined to get from one side to the other) I would recall Hoagland's keen-eyed line: "They don't feel that the contest is unfair; they keep plugging, rolling like sailorly souls — a bobbing, infirm gait, a brave, sea-legged momentum — stopping occasionally to study the lay of the land." Invariably when I'd stop to give one a lift to the side for which it was headed, it would tuck in its head until only the tiny snout was visible. Very seldom did I wait for its head to protrude, and for it to move along in its ponderous way. The lure of the open road was stronger than my curiosity about turtles. As I pedaled northward, I also recalled that light-hearted quatrain by Ogden Nash:

> The turtle lives 'twixt plated decks
> Which practically conceal its sex.
> I think it clever of the turtle
> In such a fix to be so fertile.

I realize assuring a few fertile, courageous, self-contained turtles safe passage will not alter very much the cosmic scheme of things, but every little bit helps. Somehow, the cycling seemed easier for a few miles after a gentle rescue or two. A turtle assisted is a conscience eased.

For those cyclists and other readers who may be anxious by now to get on with the story of my trip north rather than reading cute quatrains about turtles, allow me just one more dog story. As I recalled the turtle ditty, I remembered an anecdote about that late humorist who produced more than 20 volumes of verse.

It seems an admirer of Nash's work owned a dog who chewed up a copy of one of the poet's book of verses. Not only had it been autographed, but it was also out of print. The book-loving dog owner finally located another copy of the book and sent it to Nash, requesting another autographed copy. The book was returned with the dedication: "To Tom Carlson or his dog — depending on whose taste it best suits."

Let's hope this little book isn't going to the dogs!

Chapter Ten

Cars, Trucks and Other Highway Hazards

People on horses look better than they are.
People in cars look worse than they are.

—Marya Mannes
More in Anger

Every novice highway cyclist knows that feeling — stomach tightening — as anything motor-driven approaches from behind. You edge your way to the right, hugging the white line, tightening your grip on the bars, peering into your rearview mirror. Whether projecting like a dentist's mirrored probe from your helmet or a Cyclops eye mounted on your left handlebar, it becomes your most valued accessory. Of course, your ears are perked, too.

As I wended my way north, along state and county highways and byways, from West Palm Beach to Sarnia, Ontario, I developed a keen ear for approaching traffic noises. Cars humming by become commonplace. As they passed, I would maintain my course just as unwavering as possible, spinning steadily, teeth tight. Inaudibly, I'd remind myself, again, of my pedal-driven right to my share of the road. I'm legal. Bicycles have just as much business on this road as do cars and trucks, etc., etc. But one wishes, always, for more uncluttered room on one's right. Get as far removed as possible from internal combustioned intruders.

As the rumble of an approaching truck became louder, my knuckles would change color momentarily until the heightened threat would pass. Cars whine, then swish by, almost always audibly indistinguishable from one another, it seemed. But trucks are more assertive, more expressive. Big trucks can intimidate. It's not merely their approaching rumble; it's also their windy wakes as they swoop by that can be particularly unnerving.

However, we spinning lovers of the open road soon learn how to cope. Our peace of mind depends upon the size of the vehicle and its mission. Mission? That's right. In my opinion, you're as safe on the road with other vehicles as the importance of their missions is to them.

Most overland haulers — moving vans, tractor-trailers, machinery haulers, doublewide home carriers — have only one object in mind. They want to get from Point A to Point B as quickly and safely as the law allows. Time is of the essence. Professional truck drivers not only are trained for their particular jobs, but they quickly acquire experience, because for many of them, the less time on the road hauling a particular load, the more money in their pockets. Why should cyclists care? Only to understand why overland truckers may appear relatively indifferent to bicycles along the road as they roar by. In my experience, most cars will ease a foot or two to the left if they have the room as they pass. Big trucks seem to thunder by right on course, not yielding any more than is absolutely necessary to miss you.

A FALLEN ROCK Zone is not as dangerous for cyclists passing through eastern Kentucky as are heavily-laden coal trucks hurtling along the highway.

Most truckers I've chatted with in truck stops on my way north are impatient with cyclists who insist on crowding them on the road. Here's how one roadmaster in South Carolina phrased it: "Tell your buddies we're trying to save time and money when we're hauling. When they don't move over to the side at a stop light, or insist on blocking the way for whatever reason, well, we get pissed." He was big. Sported a heavy, black beard. Wore a T-shirt with "Roadkill Cafe" emblazoned on it, complete with an offbeat "menu." He stabbed his coffee cup spoon across the table at me for emphasis. I got the point.

The phrase, "Man, he blew me away," suddenly surfaced in my mind. I recalled a motorist friend uttering that complaint after he had been outgunned by another driver with more horsepower at a traffic intersection as a stoplight changed from red to green. However, from a cyclist's vantage point along the road's edge as an 18-wheeled behemoth roars by, being blown away carries an acutely literal meaning. The direction in which one is blown varies with the kind of truck that passes.

To lean on a nautical metaphor, most alert touring cyclists have felt the bow wake of a big truck as it passes at cruising speed less than three feet away. That is, the hapless cyclist senses the relatively gentle push of air created by the truck's huge prow of radiator, windshield, and fenders moving at maximum allowable highway speed. Then comes a kind of momentary pocket of calm. There's no air resistance at all, particularly if the biker has been pedaling in a cross or head wind which has been blocked momentarily by the passing vehicle. It can feel like a subtle boost, an invisible hand reaching out and nudging one along. But beware! That oh-so-brief push can end abruptly. If the passing tractor is hauling a long, flat-sided box trailer, it could suck a cyclist into a disaster. As one highway trooper explained to me, the box creates a "curl." It moves from outside to inside, forming a slipstream. Race car drivers love it. The "curl" refers to that kind of a backdraft created as the vehicle moves along.

At another coffee break stop along the way, two "staties," as highway patrol troopers are called in some locales, were commenting on the finer points of highway and byway travel. They were warning me about passing trucks. "Race car drivers use slipstreams of the cars ahead of them all the time," one explained. As he chatted, I recalled a conversation with Tom Kaufman of West Palm Beach, an avid race driver of "Formula" cars. He had explained how NASCAR drivers often use this "drafting" technique, particularly if their car and one they're trying to pass are about equal in horsepower and design.

"It's called a 'slingshot pass' or a 'draft pass,'" Tom explained. "If you're running head-to-head and can't get ahead, you tuck in behind and actually pick up speed because you don't have the wind resistance of the car you're trying to pass. Then, just before you might collide, you pull out and around, passing with the momentum you've gained in his draft." Imagine the skill and timing required for that maneuver!

I certainly wasn't about to draft behind a truck, although some motorists do just that, according to the officers I was chatting with. "It's not recommended," one muttered, shaking his head at the memory of some foolhardy motorist who must have tried the illegal, but allegedly gas-saving tactic.

"What you want to watch out for is being sucked back by that 'curl' as a fast-moving, square-backed rig passes you," his partner warned.

I nodded. "I've been there," I said. It's all in going through it for the first time. One doesn't forget the sensation of being pulled toward the road just after the rear end of the trailer goes by. Sometimes, two trucks will seem to team up in tandem, one behind the other. I shiver even as I write this at the prospect of an unwary cyclist not realizing the danger lurking in the invisible, but potentially deadly curl. Then, after momentarily being lulled by the calm air as the first tractor-trailer passes, the cyclist could suddenly being jerked out into the path of the following tractor-trailer. I have felt the tug of a curl as trucks passed me on my trip north, but I quickly learned what to expect, and to brace myself for the inevitable tug of the curl. Fortunately, it's not the same for all trucks.

In the vicinity of Lake Okeechobee where I rode to gain some experience for extended highway travel before heading north, sugar cane-hauling trucks were common. They always seemed to me to be the most anxious to get where they were going, usually from the field to the cane-crushing mill during harvest times. Of course, a cyclist's nose should warn him when cane trucks are approaching. Cane fields are burned when sugar-laden stalks are ready for the mill. The burning not only clears away the underbrush for the harvesters, either human cutters or machines, but the heat also drives the sugar sap up the stalks. Haulers try to tote the cut cane from the fields to the mills within 24 hours after it has been harvested. Their trucks reek of smoke as they pass, their 22-ft cagelike boxes packed full of cane stalks, rattling along as fast as the law allows toward their destinations. If possible, I usually would get off the road into the grass when they went by. Fortunately, their wire mesh, open-topped trailers didn't create the infamous curl, but there were no shoulders in many areas where I rode, getting into shape for my upcountry trek, so just getting out of the way was the safest move.

Of course the burning of the cane fields sometimes drives the poor little critters who have made homes in the underbrush out into the roads. No, it's not a mass of slithering snakes one encounters, but the unpleasant odor of singed fur sometimes lingers (the small, brown marsh rabbits abound in the cane fields), and too many inert carcasses lie along the highway. Ah, the unrealized, ugly byproducts of man's taste for sweets.

The long, smooth-sided tractor-trailers were encountered mostly on the highways heading up the east coast of Florida. More often than not, if they could not swing out around me because of oncoming traffic or other vehicles around them, they would sound their distinctive air horns if they felt I might be too close to their paths of travel. A couple of short truck horn blasts would galvanize me into reaching for my brakes and getting off the road if necessary. I'd try to keep a sharp eye out as heavier traffic approached on the oncoming lane as well as that coming up behind me. If I was out too far in the road, a trucker would give a long blast. That meant MOVE OVER NOW! I moved.

As I rode up through Georgia, I passed through onion-growing country. There, I encountered cagelike trailers similar to those of the cane haulers, but of an entirely different odor. Those Vadallia onions were so sweet to the taste, I picked up a few that had spilled from the trucks and nibbled on them as I rode along. Not as sweet as an apple, but not a trace of cane smoke around.

Logging trucks were constant potential threats as I traveled through Georgia and South Carolina. But because of their design and for strictly personal reasons, I enjoyed their brief, thundering-by company. First, their contours of stacked logs didn't create the potentially deadly curls as they rumbled by. I did conjure brief, frightening fantasies of their bindings breaking as they passed, spilling out timber to wipe me off the road. But that never happened. Second, their sometimes pungent odor of pine sap recalled my father's youth, and his love for the woods as the son of a lumber camp foreman in northern Michigan and Canada. When I was 12 and a native of Chicago, we vacationed to Sault St. Marie, Ontario, visiting distant relatives. That fragrant odor of pine forests still lingers in my memory.

Now coal trucks are a different story. While climbing the narrow, winding roads through the Appalachian Mountains in western Virginia and Kentucky, I grew increasingly apprehensive of coal haulers. Their massive ten wheels are capable of carrying 40 to 60 tons. According to Roosevelt Blair, a carpenter and stone mason extraordinaire who lives in Virgie, Kentucky, some drivers will illegally haul as much as 90 tons of hard coal.

Roosevelt befriended me one early June evening while he and his wife, Eva, were out for a stroll at dusk. I was looking for a place to sleep after wending my way through the two-lane highway from Elkhorn City in Southeastern Kentucky, just across the Virginia border. I had camped out the previous night in Breaks Interstate Park after leaving Route 80 in the northeastern most tip of the Jefferson National Forest.

The "Breaks" are unusual rock formations near the Russell Fork River. Prehistoric Indian artifacts abound there. The view from the lodge restaurant, 2500 feet above the river bed, is as picturesque as any in the Cumberland Mountains, I was told. Low-hanging wisps of clouds drifted down the valley below where the river ribboned between the abrupt, rugged outcropping of the Breaks. However, once the sun fell below the peaks in that country, darkness descended quickly, so I left the breathtaking view to get squared away for the night.

It had been a difficult day of winding west along Route 197 to Shelby Gap, then north on 119 to Virgie. I had hoped to get to Pikeville along back roads, but the coal trucks kept roaring past, forcing me to crouch along the edge of the road, sometimes with my back almost to the rising rock behind me. It hadn't been easy, but I had no choice. I pushed on in spurts between coal trucks.

Roosevelt and Eva told me there were no hotel or motel accommodations nearby, but I was welcome to stay at their house. Not wanting to intrude, I opted for their front lawn, just a few steps from the main street running through town. I could have pitched my tent in their back yard, but Monique, their protective half-wolf dog, on a wire run, seemed to object.

"She'll settle down after awhile," Roosevelt assured me, but I decided not to wake her with every turn I might make in my sleeping bag.

"That little patch between the car and that truck would be fine," I replied. I had noticed all along the way through the rural areas that no longer useable vehicles might be found anywhere. Having two on one's front lawn was not too unusual. I had already eaten dinner, but the Blairs insisted I have some coffee. As the dark deepened, I thanked them and prepared to turn in. Just as I zipped up the front flaps of my pup tent, a coal truck thundered by.

"Don't let those trucks keep you awake," Roosevelt called. "They run day and night through here." He was right. They did.

At dawn the next morning, Mr. Blair brought down a steaming cup of coffee. "Trucks bother you much?"

"No," I lied, "slept just fine."

"They haul by the ton. Mostly on contract. They own their

own rigs. Have to keep 'em running to make the payments. They get from $1.50 to maybe $4 a ton, depending on how far they deliver."

"I heard about them from the Western Cafe owner in Elkhorn," I replied. "He claimed a guy had ridden here from California on his bike, but decided to head back after getting out of the way of coal trucks for a couple of days coming through this area."

"Not surprising," Roosevelt said. "We don't see too many bike riders on the road around here. It'll get better when you hit the four-lane, Route 23, on up the road 'bout ten mile."

I couldn't wait.

A morning drizzle greeted me on my way out of Virgie. I was tempted to stop at a service station whose owner hailed me from his office doorway in the dawning light. "Got a hot cup of coffee for you," he called, holding up his cup as I pedaled by.

"Thanks, no," I waved. "I'd better keep going." That now-familiar example of the kindness of strangers kept me warm even though the rain was beginning to soak through my rain gear. So much for Ultrex by Burlington Mills. Lightweight, but far from waterproof. Fortunately, the temperature hovered in the 70s, and the sky cleared as I came to the four-lane highway 12 miles from Virgie.

Roosevelt had been right. At least I had a shoulder to lean toward on this state road where Route 23 was joined by Route 119. I hugged that shoulder all the rest of the way north to the Ohio River. I hadn't seen any of the well manicured horse farms located farther west in the famed Bluegrass State known for its Kenntucky Derby, but I was content. As I worked my way through a stack of pancakes in Pikesville, where Routes 23 and 119 were joined by State Road 80, I checked my Kentucky high-way map. Where should I head to cross the mighty Ohio, whose meandering path's most northerly point was punctuated by Cincinnati? I was well east of Interstate 75 which bisected Ohio from south to north. It headed straight to Cincinnati, which had bustled since post-colonial times as a trans-shipping center for early settlers. Now, much too bustling for a solo cyclist.

Besides, I-75, that pulsing, blue-lined artery, was out of bounds for cyclists, as are all Interstates. I chose to head north-northwest on State Road 80 until it joined Route 114. Then, at West Liberty, I'd choose an even less traveled-by pink capillary, Route 519, which would take me through the northern tip of the Daniel Boone National Forest to Morehead. From that college town, I'd pick up Route 32 to Maysville, another historic town on the Ohio, but far less metropolitan than Cincinnati. As soon as I passed through Pikesville, those rumbling coal trucks seemed less threatening as they thundered by.

I hadn't realized as I pedaled my way up Route 32 that I was entering the "Land of Covered Bridges," and I wasn't anywhere near Madison County, Iowa. Its bridges were made famous by that phenomenally best-selling novel-into-movie of 1995 starring Clint Eastwood and Meryl Streep. Too bad the Maysville-Mason County Tourism Commission couldn't have initially lured the novel's author, Robert James Waller, to their five-county region. Later, reading a delightful brochure with just the right touch of typographical whimsy promoting Maysville and its surrounding counties, I read that the land of covered bridges boasts eight of them.

The Goddard "White" Bridge over Sandlick Creek caught my eye as I headed north on Route 32 in Fleming county. Located on Maddox Road just off the highway at Goddard, it stretchs 63 feet over the creek. I was in luck because I could ride through this all-wood structure built in the mid-

NOTE THE wooden pegs in a "Kissing Bridge" in northern Kentucky.

1800s. All the rest were closed to road traffic, according to that promotional brochure I picked up in Maysville. Unfortunately, my wife wasn't riding with me on our tandem. We could have taken the hint suggested by the nickname given these picturesque structures in the horse-and-buggy days — "Kissing Bridges."

I had enjoyed photographing the covered bridge with its "tree nails" (wooden pegs joining its timbers) but had had my fill of hills and dales by the time I reached Maysville. Passing through the national forest was delightful. However, I longed to ease into my native midwestern flatland again (I was born and reared in a northwest Chicago suburb). Successfully conquering the Appalachians was heady, but enough was enough. Little did I realize that the greatest potential road hazards I would face were just ahead. They lay in waiting with steel teeth on the Maysville Bridge.

I arrived in that picturesque river city, a pioneering gateway to the West, on June 10th as the five-o'clock going-home commute was beginning to surge in both directions across the great river, from Kentucky to Aberdeen, Ohio. While waiting for the commuting traffic to slacken, I grabbed a quick meal in downtown Maysville. As I strolled through the historic district, I discovered the whole downtown area is listed in the National Register of Historic Places. Daniel Boone and Simon Kenton were among the founding fathers. That huge bridge I was fretting about crossing was named after Kenton.

I took the time to walk through most of the eight-block downtown historic district where the architectural styles range from Georgian to Greek Revival to Victorian. Even the French influence from downrivers (Ohio to Mississippi) New Orleans exerted a ornamented architecture, complete with wrought-iron railings. I vowed to return some day for a more leisurely looksee into this bustling port and marketplace. Tobacco was the king crop here. I had passed several of the 18 active warehouses on the way into town. My friendly waitress at dinner claimed Maysville was the world's second largest burley tobacco market. She was just as proud of Maysville for being singer Rosemary

Clooney's birthplace. All of us of a certain age remember her. She's still going strong, according to the waitress.

By six p.m., the two-way traffic was still heavy, and I was getting edgy. I still had no idea where I would spend the night. I wanted to find a campsite on the Ohio side before the sun dropped over the horizon. I had moteled it the night before in Morehead, so I was set on camping out. I envisioned gazing out over the bluffs of the river that evening, but first I had to transverse the bridge.

It offered only two lanes. One ran north, the other south. There was a foot-high curb which was 24 inches wide along the river edge of each lane. This ledge abutted the iron rails on either side. There was no pedestrian walkway. Compact cars and tractor-trailer trucks alike crossed the bridge using the same one-way lanes. An endless flow of traffic rumbled across the long span from both directions, halted only by traffic lights on either end. However, when the north-south traffic was halted, the east-west traffic along both the Kentucky and Ohio sides had its chance to turn left or right to cross the bridge.

There was no room for a touring cyclist alongside a tractor-trailer. And I didn't want to ask a compact car driver to drive only about 17 mph max while I rode along side until we reached the Ohio side. No, I'd have to time my passage somehow to allow me to scoot across during a lull in the vehicular flow.

I had watched the flow from street level in Maysville. I had even parked the bike and walked up along the top of the 24-inch curb to estimate how steep a climb it would be, once I was committed. I contemplated pushing the bike ahead of me or somehow dragging it behind me along the span on top of that imposing curb, but that, too, seemed not only ludicrous, but potentially very dangerous. No, by golly, I'd demand equal rights to the road for the Great Crossing. I had bowed to the authority of weight, width, roar, and rumble for 1,200 miles. I had cowered along white lines through seven states. Now, I would assert myself, claim my inalienable privilege of equal access to paved highway.

I waited patiently for what seemed hours as the bridgebound

cars and trucks shifted into lower gears in Maysville and headed up the bridge, then across and on into Ohio. Finally, a slight break in traffic opened up. I shifted into my lowest granny gear and took my place in the only available lane. It was futile to glance back. There was no room for any vehicle to pass me. Head down, I surged onward, my pink pennant waving bravely from its fiberglass wand on the rear wheel.

As I crested the top of the onramp, I thought I had it made. Now to shift into a higher gear for the straightaway across the bridge. Wait! There, not ten yards ahead of me, were gaping metallic slots in the pavement, slots too wide for *Sir Walter's* tires to negotiate. I stopped pedaling just in time to avoid disaster. Hopping off the bike, I leaped up onto the two-foot top of the curb and hauled *Sir Walter* up with me, panniers and all, my pink pennant waving frantically back and forth. I flattened myself back against the rail and hugged the bike to me. The inboard panniers hung over the curb, but with any luck, there was room for cars and trucks behind me to pass.

Nobody had honked. Nobody cursed at me as they sped by, but nobody stopped either. By the time they reached those tooth-like expansion joints, looking like huge, gaping dragons' teeth as

THERE IS no room for cyclists on the Maysville Bridge which has narrow curbs, no walkways and expansion joints with a taste for bike tires.

I gazed down and through them to the river below, the car drivers were settling into a steady pace as they crossed the bridge. Their concern was not whether they could drive over the joints. The gaps between the teeth were of no concern to them, but those same gaps would have crunched *Sir Walter's* wheels, and the fall might have broken some of my bones as well. Now what?

I tried inching along sideways, but it was impossible to keep my bike going straight ahead with both front and rear panniers bumping along the railing ahead of and behind me. I'd just have to wait for a gap in the traffic. Then, I realized another problem. I had carried the bike across the expansion joint before I hopped up out of the traffic lane, but there would be another joint on the other side of the bridge. Ah, the curse of the change of seasons, hot to cold weather. Expansion and contraction. Those joints simply didn't exist in South Florida, and I didn't recall them threatening me on the long bridge spanning the Savannah River between Georgia and South Carolina.

Then I remembered. I had noticed them as I stopped on top of that bridge to enjoy a midday view east along the flow of the stately river. No traffic on Route 301 threatened me that weekday. There were no towns bordering the river in that rural area. I had dismounted and walked *Sir Walter* diagonally across the expansion joints above the Savannah River. But that was then. This was now.

Then, unbelievably, a huge truck stopped and the driver leaned out the window. "Go ahead," he yelled. "I ride bikes, too. Those joints'll get ya."

I jumped down, swung a leg over the saddle and spurred *Sir Walter* on. I might have hit 18 mph by the time I got to the Ohio side. There were no cars coming from the Aberdeen side. I was able to swerve diagonally enough into the oncoming traffic lane to cross the northernmost of the bridge's dragon's teeth without getting nipped. As soon as there was room coming off the down-ramp, I swung off the roadway to let my savior pass. "Thanks very much!" I yelled as he passed by. My escort gave me a couple of deep-throated whoops of his airhorn and turned east up

Highway 52 towards Portsmouth. His rig carried a Georgia license plate. Ah, good old Southern hospitality. There would be one more gesture of it before night fell. I caught my breath and headed east, too, along the Ohio. The land was flat once more.

AMISH VEHICLE sign is a comfort to cyclists along southern Ohio roads because there is no recent record of a horse and buggy injuring a cyclist. I noticed the irony of seeing bullet holes in the sign because the Amish are known for their peaceful ways.

CHAPTER ELEVEN

RIDING THROUGH MY HEARTLAND

Happy the man whose wish and care
A few paternal acres bound
Content to breathe his native air.
In his own ground.

—Alexander Pope
Ode on Solitude

I was too busy escaping the gaping expansion joints to muse on the mighty river below me as I scooted across the Maysville Bridge that mid-spring evening. After my heart had quieted and I regained my breath, I paused along Route 52 between Aberdeen and Manchester, overlooking the tranquil Ohio. The sun was sinking behind me, and I was anxious to find a camp site. There stretched a plateau above the silent, dark, winding river hundreds of feet below. Again water, life's magnetic cradle, drew me to it. In the gathering evening mists, I watched coal barges move west, the deep thumping of their towboats' engines echoing up the bluff as they nudged their flat-bottomed cargoes toward Cincinnati and beyond. The state had taken its name from the river, the pulsing, arterial pathway west in colonial times. Trees from along its shores for almost a thousand miles had provided the logs for pioneer cabins. I was about to encounter one of those original symbols for settling about a mile up the road toward Manchester.

It was a two-story cabin standing as sturdy as it may have been when the logs forming its foot-thick sides were first hewn. It set back about 25 feet from the highway. Woods on a gentle rise formed a backdrop behind it. The cabin's front porch faced Route 52 and the grassy field across the black-topped highway. The field stretched for 200 yards to the edge of the bluff over the river. Logs had been hewn square and chinked to form the

THIS OHIO riverside log cabin dating back to late 1700s once was a frontier trading post.

cabin's walls. They certainly appeared to be original to my untrained eye. An electric porch light burned, but nobody answered my knocking. I leaned *Sir Walter* against the cabin's rugged side wall and walked around back. Nope, nobody home. Shadows of evening were lengthening. I made my decision. I would walk the bike to the bluff's edge directly across the road and pitch my tent under those trees to the east, high on the bluff overlooking the river. No houses were on the river side of the highway in that immediate area, but there was a picnic table and a child's swing set placed back from the cliff's edge. I had tried to get permission. It wouldn't be the first time I had trespassed in search of a few square feet to lay my head for a night.

No sooner than I had staked out my tent and settled down to a late, after-dinner snack on the nearby picnic table than a car turned into the driveway beside the cabin. Then it turned and headed across the road and down the path I had just taken, coming straight for me. Caught red-tented!

It was a mini-van. I rose, open-handed, and stepped away

from the table. I fumbled for a business card from my wallet in my shorts pocket and extended it toward the vehicle, trying not to appear furtive. The card stated that I was a licensed boat captain, specializing in deliveries and the teaching of sailing. Boats and bicycles had been my outdoor passions for 50 years. The driver stepping out of the car was maybe forty-something, casually dressed; his companion, an attractive woman about his age.

"Hi. I'm Frank Bostwick from West Palm Beach, Florida. Am I trespassing on your land?"

The man nodded. "You might say so," he replied evenly, taking the card, glancing at it. No smile yet. "I'm Wilbur Shelton. This is my wife, Mary Ellen."

"That your cabin there?"

He nodded.

"I knocked on your door before I came over," I stammered. "Nobody answered. I'll move my tent off your property if you wish, but I'll be gone by daylight. I'm headed for Michigan, to see my daughter."

Sir Walter also appeared supplicant. His humble presence prompted the usual questions and eyebrow-raising remarks. "You mean you've ridden all the way from Florida?" That broke whatever ice of indignant landowner attitude might have been crystallizing. Turned out the Sheltons had driven out from Manchester, a few miles east on Route 52, to enjoy a picnic supper on the river's bluff and to check on their second home. Almost immediately they asked me to share their supper with them. Mr. Shelton smiled easily and said it would be okay to stay where I was. No need to move. We all relaxed.

Perhaps the wide river below marked some kind of territorial line between north and south, but the same permeations of human warmth I had basked in for almost a month continued to spread around me. Good old Southern hospitality prevailed.

We shared the usual pleasantries, small talk inquiries about occupations, marital and parental status, the weather. But I was really curious about their cabin. Yes, it had been restored to its original appearance as much as possible. The cabin measured 32 by 25 feet. The Sheltons had purchased it two years before. Yes, those were the original logs. They had discovered them under two layers of latter-day wood siding and decided to restore as much of the cabin's original look as was practical. Indoor plumbing and piped-in water had been added before the Sheltons picked up the title. Those modern conveniences were kept, of course. Their diligent research into deeds in the county courthouse, and earlier documents housed in state archives in Columbus, revealed that it was built back in 1793!

"You might have noticed there are two sections to the place," Mr. Shelton explained. "We discovered some siding on the back that resembled what might have been a store front. Then, we noticed what once was a road behind the house. Perhaps the place was originally a general store or trading post of some kind long before the present road was cut through where Route 52 now runs."

I wondered if there were any ghosts of irate Indians or plundering pioneers past hanging around, but didn't ask.

By the time we had finished eating the sun had set, and lights were winking on along the river. When the trees first had been felled for the Sheltons' weekend/vacation home, only campfires would have appeared along the mighty Ohio. Mosquitos began to buzz around us, and we bid each other adieu. We had chatted longer than expected. The Sheltons' daughter, Sarah, was to begin college that fall at Antioch in Yellow Springs; I had taught for six years at Kalamazoo College in Michigan, another highly regarded private four-year school, so we discussed that big first step of leaving home and how traumatic it could be for both students and parents.

A short time later, as I zipped out the night insects and listened to the lonely sound of a hooting owl in the woods behind me, I thought about the Sheltons' cabin, turning 200 that year. How many strangers had received some form of comfort or assistance as they traveled west along the Ohio past that cabin door, particularly if it had been a general store or trading post of some kind? Unlike a college-bound student, those folks passing through in the early 18th and 19th centuries would probably never return as they headed west. Ours always has been a nation of travelers. In T.S. Eliot's words, home is merely where one starts from.

As I stood up in front of my trespassing pup tent the next dawn to stretch and gaze down on the river from the bluff, I could barely see across the dark water. It was engulfed by a heavy, slowly rising mist. Ghostlike, moving slowly, some of the Ohio's most ponderous travelers glided silently below in the channel along the opposite shore. I counted a string of 15 barges being pushed by a thumping towboat. They were lashed three abreast and extended five deep from stem to stern — one huge moving mass of waterborne freight. I had learned the night before while eating that early supper in a downtown Maysville restaurant that the usual barge cargoes were either coal, crushed stone, or scrap iron. How on earth did a towboat skipper stop a moving behemoth like that, let alone turn it away from unexpected danger in an emergency? As I packed up *Sir Walter*, I was thankful for being able to travel light, not to be responsible for controlling momentum at its most awesome.

My momentum was psychological. I, too, was unswerving in my desire to complete my journey, to reach my goal. Concern with time again, present time. It pressed in on me. I wanted to get there just as soon as I could. I'd been on my way for almost a month, and while the lure of the open road was still there, I was ready to send post cards from Canada to biking friends back in South Florida. The mountains were behind us. *Sir Walter* and I had traveled safely through seven states. Only Ohio and the lower half of Michigan were left to challenge us, but it was merely the benign threat of distance and possibly rainy weather, not that of unknown elevations sprouting hairpin turns, or of surprised dogs and coal trucks driven by clock-watching owners or lessees.

That morning, as the fog lifted, we headed east to Manchester, then north on Route 136 to pick up Route 41. I stopped to enjoy a heaping plate of pancakes in West Union.

Forty-one would take us all the way to Greenfield.

I would continue to choose those north-south pink lines on road maps. They were paved. Gray lines might be unpaved, but the double-red (four-lane, divided) ones and the big blue Interstates would be avoided. The four-laners could be tolerated, and sometimes unavoidable around larger cities, but Interstates were off limits to cyclists. Who cared? We preferred the pink routes. They were friendliest. If they had tiny green dots paralleling them, indicating a "scenic" route, they were even more welcome. Fortunately, the relatively flat terrain of the beckoning Midwest lent itself to cyclist-friendlier roads. We bypassed Cincinnati and Dayton to the west by wide margins and Columbus, the state's capital to the east, also would be shunned. We would get our fill of big cities, Toledo and Detroit, on our way to my daughter's home in Pt. Huron.

We didn't quite make Greenfield as the sun was dropping in the west. This night, I knocked on William Gregg's door on the Salem Road, south of Greenfield, for permission to sleep down at the end of his property along the road. With the briefest of formalities, he said sure, but I had one more question. "Do you have a dog?"

"Only this little one," he pointed to a mixed breed, all black, wagging its tail at his feet.

"Might he bark at the tent during the night if you let him out?"

"Not this one. He doesn't roam at night. Waits 'til I'm up in the morning."

I thanked Mr. Gregg, patted his tail-wagging companion for a moment, just to let him know what I smelled like, and rolled *Sir Walter* back down to the edge of the road near the garage.

I rested peacefully that night. *Sir Walter* and I had covered 68 miles during the day, the longest since that first, humid 73-mile day to Fort Pierce from West Palm Beach.

On the way into Greenfield the next day for breakfast, my front derailleur broke. That's the open-ended guide through which the drive chain passes before it grabs the teeth on one of three gears on the chain ring. Another derailleur on the bike's frame rear wheel can move that drive chain onto six different positions offered by free wheels (gear sprockets) of various diameters on the rear wheel hub. That fractured front chain guide meant that I would be unable to shift from one gear to another without manually reaching down to move the chain from one sprocket to another. That would be a foolhardy move while underway. A finger caught between a chain link and a gear tooth could delay the trip painfully while a mangled finger healed. No, I'd stick to one sprocket forward to see how it worked out for awhile. I'd still have a choice of six different gearing combinations. Had that front derailleur broken in the mountains... But it hadn't.

Those Illinois flatlands where I had learned to cycle in my childhood were part of the breadbasket vista before me now in Ohio and Michigan. Endless fields of grains and corn and pastures galore for four-footed meat-producers were emerging before me as I rode north. I never did get that derailleur replaced. Time spent for a replacement seemed less important than time spent spinning along, ever nearer to my goal.

Nature, indifferent to humankind, had certainly seemed benevolent to me along the way. Except for that persistent north wind in northern Florida and part of a day of rain in Kentucky, I had enjoyed smooth riding, weatherwise. Now, as I rode along those arrowlike north-south routes toward Toledo, the prevailing westerlies sometimes swung south, providing a welcome boost on my port quarter. Overcast skies loomed on Tuesday, June 14 as I rode up State Route 68 toward Findlay. During an early supper of fried chicken, potatoes, a side dish of carrots, and two salad bar refills, I watched the weather report on TV. A tornado watch was out for the area. I chose a motel at sundown after slipping under Interstate 75 and heading west to Route 235, another one of those friendly pink highways heading due north. My tenting had been relatively tranquil up to now. Why worry about being whirled away in a twister?

Stopping at motels one of every three nights kept me from

appearing too roadworn for mingling with polite society. I could trim my beard and mustache, soak in a hot tub; there is no substitute for that kind of relaxation after a day of steady spinning. In fact, Edmund Wilson once stated, "I have had a good many more uplifting thoughts, creative and expansive visions while soaking in comfortable baths in well-equipped American bathrooms than I ever had in any cathedral." I have a feeling old iconoclastic Edmund was not referring to the budget motels I chose, but I also had no way to compare my surroundings with cathedrals either. A church in every little community for sure, but cathedrals, no.

Motels also offered running water in useful containers, like wash basins and bathtubs. Of course I never washed clothes in that other essential container, but it did provide the pause that refreshes in much more relaxed positions than modern, urban man is used to if caught suddenly outdoors by an urgent call of nature. How we North American folk, still strongly influenced by the Puritan ethic, do avoid direct discussion of bodily functions. I, too, choose to.

Washing clothes while bike touring solo can present problems, but motels have answers to at least half the problem. They provide plenty of water, hot and cold, but drying clothes can be frustrating. Washing my shirts, shorts, skivvies and socks were always the first tasks I tackled after arriving at a motel. Then I'd spread the stuff around to dry as quickly as possible. Cheaper motels have more dusty window curtain rods, but I learned to wipe them off before draping things on them. Most motels these days have sealed windows because of our dedication to air-conditioning, but things do dry out pretty well overnight. I recall only one unfortunate impromptu "laundry" incident.

Way back in Green Cove, Florida, I had stopped in a rather creepy motel. The owner had combined a half-hearted antique business with the motel. The registration desk was surrounded by antiques. In fact, it was situated right in the middle of a whole room of antiquated stuff that reminded me of that old adage: One man's junk is another man's treasure. Many of these "treasures" had found their way to the motel's guest rooms. Let's say the rooms were furnished eclectically. That is, a free selection from diverse sources.

Into one of those imaginatively furnished rooms I lugged *Sir Walter* and unloaded my dirty clothes. The pile included one of two pairs of wool socks I carried in the panniers. I have found that, for me, wool socks are the best to wear while cycling. They seem to "wick off" the moisture and keep my feet in better shape. They don't dry as quickly as cotton socks so I'd always wash them first and look for the best place to dry them. Usually they're draped over a lampshade with the light bulb turned on. On this particular occasion, I stretched my favorite pair of squeezed-as-dry-as-possible wool socks across an eclectic lampshade that seemed to be strong enough to support them. After I had washed the rest of my sweaty stuff and spread it out to dry, I headed for the shower. About halfway through a particularly enjoyable scrub, I caught the smell of burning wool. Half the lamp shade had simply collapsed, dropping a sock on the hot bulb. Before I could get the fallen sock off the bulb, a hole about the size of a half-dollar had been burned in its instep. After I dried off and dressed, I inspected the damaged sock. Fortunately, the ensuing smoke had not set off an alarm. The sock was saveable. I would darn it.

The next day, I searched for darning needles in stores along the way north. They weren't as easy to find as I had thought, but finally I located one in a "dollar store," along with a skein of white yarn which I laboriously rolled into a ball. The ensuing patch would have been a lot easier to weave if I had had a wooden darner. I wasn't shopping for one of those. Didn't want to carry it. I'd just improvise. I had watched my mom darn my older sister Jean's and my socks during the Depression years as I was growing up. Those were the days when women were knitting more than they seem to do today. Most kids in my neighborhood wore wool socks, especially through Chicago's winters. Mine went clear up above my knees and tucked under the elastic band around the bottom rim of my knickers.

As I struggled to patch up that scorched wool sock the following night, camping out along the highway, so many childhood memories rushed back. I was particularly caught up in the flashback to ice-skating days on a flooded and frozen football-field-turned-ice-rink in Olympia Park in Edison Park, the northwestern most suburb of Chicago where I grew up. After skating around the man-made pond until our toes and fingers were numb, we'd clump up the wooden ramp from the ice to the wooden shack on our skates. Our damp outer garments and wet wool mittens would steam up as we moved them as close as we dared to the pot-bellied wood stove in the warming shack. The woolly odor of the drying garments, socks, and mittens from a cold, long-ago February day engulfed me that humid May evening along the road north as I sat, cross-legged, darning my sock. I reached up and touched my left ear. It had been frostbitten when I loaned my earmuffs to a young girl my age one bitter cold day on that windswept midwestern ice rink. Funny, I couldn't even recall the girl's name now, in this time-warped, sultry Florida evening, weaving the patch. Oh, she had made my heart beat faster that winter day as I insisted she keep wearing them as we whirled around the rink together, laughing. I still recalled the delicious thrill of their warmth as she handed them back to me when her mother came to pick her up in their car, a Chevy. That left ear still sticks out more than my right; bigger, too. Ah, the silly chivalry of youth. What was that dark-haired beauty's name?

For several alternate days on the road after that darning evening, when I'd pull on the imperfectly patched sock, I'd grin and touch my ear. Bike touring has a way of churning up childhood interludes. Home is where one starts from. Now I was moving toward the big cities of Toledo and Detroit. I'd prefer to skirt them, but the shortest distance between two points is that proverbial straight line. I decided to risk riding through the vortex of compacted big city dangers, spawned by auto-manufacturing and related industries, to reach my upcountry goal as quickly as possible — Port Huron and across to Canada.

Chapter Twelve

Bodiless Silk and Big City Blight

Nowadays almost all man's improvements, so called, as the building of houses and the cutting down of the forest and of all large trees, simply deform the landscape, and make it more and more tame and cheap.

—Thoreau
Walden

That Big Sky feeling claimed by the plains states farther west took over, almost lifting me out of the saddle as I hopscotched north through Ohio — Manchester to Greenfield, Greenfield to Marysville, Marysville to Findlay. The lyrics of "America, the Beautiful" kept rising up within me from the countryside. The majesty of mist-shrouded Smokies had brushed my brow instead of the Rockies' purple splendor, but mountains are awesome, regardless of hue. Now I was spinning through some waving fields of grain, Kansas-claimed, perhaps, but beside me now, feeling the bodiless silk of wind on grass, sensuality undulating in the deepening springtime.

Sir Walter and I rejoiced in God's shedding light, that is, once we turned west on Route 159 under Interstate I-75 north of Findlay in search of a pink road heading up and around Bowling Green. Route 186 helped us join up with 235. From then on, we cruised north in close harmony with the land, and crowned our good with brotherhood for all other lucky humans feeling the pulse of our nation's flat, lush heartland. A glance at our road map, though, warned us of the clogged arteries ahead as we cycled toward Toledo. Bypassing was as much on our mind as it might be for any heart patient. We were headed for Detroit and Henry Ford's industrial legacy, the auto making megalopolis of the world. We wanted to keep our touring stress level as low as possible.

There's a saying in Michigan about the auto making business, "When Detroit sneezes, the whole state catches cold." I'm sure sniffles spread rapidly in Ohio as well if the auto making pace falters. In fact, the permanent effects of a related virus, planned obsolescence, have spread throughout our entire land. I was acutely aware of it as I rode upcountry through the back roads. Dead cars were everywhere. I pitched my pup tent between two of them in Roosevelt Blair's front yard in Virgie, Kentucky. One could have been brought to life with major surgery, but the other was long gone.

Just before I came to Mr. Gregg's home on the Salem Road south of Greenfield, where I would pitch my tent for the final night on the trip north, I encountered an appalling assemblage of abandoned cars near a deserted farmstead. There lay at least an acre of rusting, four-wheeled skeletons. Weeds were sprouting merrily up through ruptured bumpers, broken windows, smashed windshields. No human activity was evident. It was an abandoned auto graveyard. Most dead cars along back roads seemed to have died alone, not even having the comfort of other metallic corpses nearby. At least these had been gathered together.

One waitress in a roadside cafe in eastern Kentucky had offered one excuse for folks hanging on to the dead cars strewn around in a lot next to her place of business: "You never know when somebody might come along and pay you for one."

Probably nothing short of a dire national defense emergency requiring the gathering and processing of scrap metal throughout the country would make any environmental improvement involving junk cars. One poem I tried to memorize as I rode along upcountry offered some comforting perspective. The poem was E.E. Cummings' "O sweet spontaneous earth" which begins with that line. Another line, while not referring specifically to dead cars, makes the point: "...how often has the naughty thumb/ of science prodded thy beauty..." Too often. However, the poem ends on an uplifting note: "thou answerest/them only with/ spring."

Unfortunately, many, many springs are needed to replace junked vehicles with elements of natural life. Dead cars and trucks continued to dot the countryside as we spun through Bowling Green and charged ahead toward the Maumee River. We resigned ourselves to a double-redlined divided highway, Route 25 which ran parallel to Interstate 75 then to the western thruway around Toledo, Interstate 475.

Divided highways are a mixed blessing for touring cyclists. We usually have more room on the right-hand side of the white line which marks the lane from the shoulder. But all that noise of whizzing traffic coupled with the shimmer of hot concrete is depressing, and when we strike those deep, indented lines imbedded in the concrete at intervals to jar motorists awake should they doze and swerve to the edge of the highway, we are really jarred. Nothing's perfect.

There was room to avoid the expansion joints on the Maumee River bridge, but after we crossed it, we ducked under the east-west Interstate 80-90, and tried to find quieter, inner-city streets. We found them, but their grim squalor heightened the tension.

I ducked into a restaurant for a quick sandwich, choosing a booth near the entrance where I could keep an eye on loaded *Sir Walter*. I always tethered him with a steel cable and lock around a steel post, but there was no way to lock up the panniers stuffed with clothes and other touring gear. The waitress understood my urgency as I scanned the menu, "Which is the quickest meal to serve, young lady?" I kept one eye peeled toward the bike.

"Hamburger's the quickest, sir." She nodded toward the bike. "Looks like you're traveling. Just keep moving through the downtown area and you'll be all right." She paused and grinned, shrugging her shoulders, "I think." The service was quick, the hamburger greasy, and its aftertaste lingered for miles down Toledo's mean streets.

I had only one really startling moment after bolting my lunch and getting underway; perhaps it was my overactive imagination. I had just navigated under an especially deep-dipping underpass. Traffic rumbled not only beside me, but overhead as well. I was struggling up the street, trying to avoid some old streetcar tracks and their attendant grooves, wishing I had stopped somewhere to have that broken front derailleur fixed. I decided to find a side street heading north to get out of the heavy traffic flow. I recall it was near the University of Toledo.

As I rounded a corner, there, stretched out flat in the sparse grass along the curb, were twenty or more small children, half naked, all screaming. For a horrible instant, I thought I had happened upon an in-progress drive-by shooting of some kind. Then I spotted the source of their high-pitched cries up on the sidewalk. Their day-camp counselor was getting ready to sprinkle them with a garden hose to cool them off. She had commanded in a loud voice for them to lie flat on the grass to keep them from running into the street.

I had all I could do to keep from laughing out loud at my paranoia. This was a summertime neighborhood, and folks were coping as best they could. The youngsters were thoroughly enjoying themselves, particularly when the counselor announced that the kid who wiggled the least could have a turn squirting the others. I dismounted and watched. Their glee was spontaneous, their cries full of pleasure, not pain. After they had enjoyed their playful dousing, their counselor lined them up, two by two, to step off to their next activity, and I headed for mine. The afternoon was late, and I was about to cross the state line into Michigan.

I decided to motel it that night along Route 24 in Monroe, along Telegraph Road. It ran parallel to Interstate 75, just west of the rumbling thruway. Before us in the distance loomed Detroit. More than a day's ride beyond lay Port Huron, and across the wide St. Clair River was Sarnia, Ontario. On the morrow, I would take as direct a route as possible along Lake Erie, through Detroit's heart, then along Lake St. Clair's edge to the river again and on to the very southern tip of Lake Huron. I felt more uneasy riding toward Detroit than I had at any time during the past 30 days on the road. Some big city dwellers do engage in dangerous activities, especially to unsuspecting passersby. Pressures of big city living occasionally trigger unexpected actions and reactions. I was an experienced city dweller. I had spent my first 24 years in Chicago. I knew which neighborhoods of the Windy City to avoid, but Detroit was not my territory. On the morrow, I would have no car windows to lock, no way to speed away from an unpleasant situation. I would be exposed to all the elements, both human and inhuman, as I cycled the shortest distance possible to pass through unknown urban territory.

As I continued on Route 24, I figured I'd ask some cyclists which was the best motel to stay in overnight. There certainly didn't seem to be any place to camp out. Traffic was heavy. I did pass a huge cemetery and watched two cyclists turn into it through some heavy iron gates. They appeared to be casual bike riders, out for an early evening ride. I had read somewhere that cemeteries were great places in which to camp overnight. Available rest rooms, green grass galore, nice trees — but get permission from the local authorities. The unique request would startle them at first, but when they realized that you were concerned with being undisturbed, the same as the folks' remains they were overseeing, so to speak, what better place could a weary traveler select than a cemetery?

I had always been at ease in cemeteries. I am fascinated by the grave markers for purely historical reasons. Isn't it always fun to find the oldest date on a tombstone, and imagine what the countryside was like at the time of that resident's birth? Besides, I am convinced that we are spiritual beings, and when this Great Adventure is over, we do not remain inside our bodies, but travel to some other place in some other form. Ashes to ashes, dust to dust; why should one be fearful of graveyards? As I passed through the back roads from the South, I rode past dozens of cemeteries, large and small.

Among the saddest roadside sights I recall were in South Carolina, where I pedaled past two well-built, well-kept two-story frame houses, side by side, set back maybe 200 feet from the highway. Both were painted white with dark green trim.

They were very similar architecturally, as though they had been built at about the same time. They stood empty. Between them was a tiny family cemetery with a wrought-iron fence surrounding it. Inside was a handful of graves. The grass inside and around the houses had not been mowed recently. FOR SALE signs were displayed on both homes. Who would buy them with that cemetery smack dab between them? Isn't some kind of special permission needed to move graves? Those tombstones seemed so lonely. Imagine the difficulty of moving away from that lovely, wooded rural homestead. I still recall the scene vividly.

No, I didn't sleep in that Michigan graveyard that night. I figured that in this relatively metropolitan setting, some policeman or security guard would run me out. Besides, that iron gate had to be swung closed and locked at night. I guess being locked inside would tend to restrict one's departing hour somewhat. But there are beautiful old trees in most older cemeteries under which to pitch a tent. They stand away from the graves, and murmur musically at night, particularly if they are conifers.

Two passing cyclists near Monroe did suggest one place to sleep. We had stopped at a traffic intersection together. I was going straight ahead. They were turning right. They wore helmets; looked like fairly serious male riders in their thirties. "Excuse me, but is there a fairly reasonable, nearby motel you would recommend for an overnight stay?" I asked as the light changed.

"Yeah," replied one. "The Crown Motel, about a mile ahead."

His companion half turned as if to question his advice, but then shrugged, and they both pedaled away. No questions to me about where I was headed, where I had been. Big city dwellers don't usually like to appear too interested in strangers, even though they're riding a loaded touring bike and the dwellers are cyclists, too. Perhaps it has to do with population densities.

I found the Crown with no problem, but it looked transient, traffic-worn. I stopped, parked the bike, locked it and opened the door to a small, empty lobby. A tiny window, shut, opened into what appeared to be the motel office. Just before I reached over to ring for the clerk, I noticed a red piece of paper, stationery-sized, tacked just below the sign containing the printed room rates. It stated in block letters in black crayon: SHORT STAY (TWO HRS) $15. The regular rates were $30. I decided to pedal on down the road to find a, well, more family-oriented motel with guests at least staying overnight. Less than a mile up the road I found one — the Sunset Motel.

As I walked up to the entrance I saw what seemed to be the place to register. It was another small window resembling a movie theater's ticket booth with heavy glass between me and the middle-aged, suspendered man behind it. Could it be bullet-proof? The thought vanished as I saw the scene behind him. Back of the registration counter in his tiny booth was the open door to the kitchen of the home attached to the motel. Apparently he had arisen from a chair nearest the booth to serve me. There behind him around an ample, circular table sat four other middle-aged men, looking at the cards just dealt to them. They arranged them, then fiddled with the poker chips in front of them as I filled out the registration form and shoved my credit card through the cuticle cut in the thick glass. $27.50 for the night. Beat the Crown's price, and no cut rates for two-hour stopovers were advertised on handwritten signs. The man hadn't seen my bike, so there were none of the usual questions. I requested a pre-dawn wakeup call. "Sure," he grunted. "Gettin' an early start, eh?"

"Yeah, got a big day tomorrow."

"Okay have a good one," and he turned back to his game, closing the narrow door to the booth behind him. I wheeled *Sir Walter* to my assigned room. The motel had been built before air conditioning and sealed windows were prerequisites for such structures. An a/c unit was stuck in one small, wooden-framed window. The other window in the room actually opened when I tried it. I chose to lock it again and flipped on the a/c. The TV set must have been among the very first color sets to replace black-and-white, but it worked. Hey, cable! The room was spotless, no cigarette smoke smell although no "no smoking" signs were visible.

I relaxed and surfed the stations. No remote, of course. I had to turn the dial. What should I happen upon but *Deliverance* with Burt Reynolds and Jon Voight. Why, if I could stay awake long enough, I might catch a glimpse of James Dickey, playing the part of the sheriff. He had told me his first (and last) acting role came up after the crew had begun shooting on location in Georgia. Dickey explained the director was concerned about a tight budget, and signed on Dickey within two days of the shooting of the scene. He wasn't bad in the role. Certainly had an authentic southern drawl, and he knew the part cold. After all, he had written the book, invented the characters. I managed to stay awake until after Sheriff Dickey's final scene, staggered to the set, clicked it off and fell back into bed. I slept soundly that night. Of course the drone of passing cars was always present, but at least there appeared to be no comings and goings from nearby rooms.

I was on the road the next morning as dawn broke. Even that early, the trucks were rumbling by. I chose to stay on Route 24, a redliner running north-by-northeast. It paralleled the blue-lined I-75 heading directly into the Motor City's bowels. Near the mammoth intersection of I-75 with I-275, I stopped for breakfast. I asked a trucker sitting next to me at the counter what would be the most direct secondary route through the city. He turned to check with the trucker next to him and nodded.

"Get as far north as you can on from Fort Street, then bear east to West Jefferson Avenue. You'll be as close as you can get to the Detroit River," he said. "That'll take you right downtown, then stay on that street — it changes to East Jefferson — and you'll be okay" He explained that the river marks the U.S.-Canadian border where Windsor nudges up to Detroit. There visitors can enjoy Motown's crown jewel, the Renaissance Center, immediately northeast of the Detroit-Windsor tunnel under the river, but I was not to sample its offerings this trip. I didn't even hesitate for a prayer-stop at the historic Mariner's Church.

As I left the counter of the restaurant, the smiling waitress leaned over and squeezed my hand. "Just keep moving. I'll be praying for you." I gave her a weak smile and a strong tip and headed into the gauntlet with imaginary opponents on either side, ready to swing at us as we passed.

West Jefferson wasn't all that bad until we passed the famed River Rouge plant. Beyond those heavy iron entrance gates were assembly lines which had shaped the world standard for mass production of automobiles in the 1920s and 1930s. To the west, beyond its huge gates and ribbons of railroad switching tracks running into the plant, stretched the most desolate inner city vistas I had ever experienced. Buildings on the west side of the road were being razed, I assumed. Certainly that area of Detroit hadn't suffered an aerial bombardment, but it seemed so to me. However, I wasn't stopping to find out. I tried to time my pace to avoid stopping at traffic lights. Strangely, there weren't too many people on the street just hanging out. A couple of bars were flashing "Open" signs amid the rubble of tumbling-down buildings, but that seemed about all.

Suddenly I arrived at Randolph and Jefferson streets, the very center of the downtown area. Now the upscale stores appeared and decay dropped away. Traffic was heavier, but pedestrians were scurrying to and fro. A good sign. I had made it safely through no-bike's land. Mid-morning was warming up and, aside from needing a pit stop, I was intact.

Now East Jefferson Avenue beckoned. Weathered brick and frame buildings of the older city still loomed, but at least they were not crumbling. Finally, a McDonald's golden arch appeared. I headed directly for it. After securing *Sir Walter* to a handicapped parking signpost, I dashed inside, heading straight for the restrooms sign. The damn door was locked! I rushed to the counter. There behind a thick plastic shield were the food servers. "Gotta use the john," I called. "Do I need a key?"

"Nope, we'll buzz you in but you're supposed to order first."

"Please! Buzz me in," I grimaced, removing my bike helmet and stripping off my gloves.

"Oh, go ahead," a burly employee waved, reading my urgent frown. "Forget your order for now."

As I approached the restrooms the buzzer sounded, and I hurried through the heavy door marked "Men." During the long pause that really refreshed, I mused upon the signs I had passed on the restroom doors. "No more than one person allowed at a time. Strictly enforced." I guess I had stopped in a popular part of the "needles" district where drugs and cash exchanges flowed freely. Well, not in McDonald's restrooms, by golly. I looked around the tiled room. Really no place to hide a stash either. I didn't stop to look in the stalls, but perhaps the lids on the toilet tanks were bolted down, too. Who knows?

When I sauntered back to the counter, trying to look the seasoned traveler, I suddenly thought of *Sir Walter* waiting patiently in the morning sunshine. I glanced over my shoulder. Everything seemed intact.

"Gimme a Big Mac, a Coke and fries," I called, not realizing I could speak in normal tones through a hole in the plastic window. I pushed two dollar bills into the tray in the turnstile at counter level. Almost immediately the turnstile whirled around with my change. Nobody else came into the line before my brunch was served. It arrived by turnstile, a kind of holdup-resistant lazy Susan, packaged as only fast food is. I wolfed down the burger and fries, swigged the soft drink and was out of there. Downtown Detroit is a great place to be from for a touring cyclist, particularly along that desolate stretch of West Jefferson, where mass production sprawled and smudged the urban landscape forever.

My uneasy feeling for my personal safety riding through the bowels of Detroit that June 15th was not enhanced by the weather. The hottest day of the year was reported, but we kept spinning. By early afternoon, we had reached Detroit's North Shore. East Jefferson had turned into Lake Shore Drive as *Sir Walter* and I settled into an easier pace, both mentally and physically. Blue-lined I-94, named the Edsel Ford Freeway in that area, was a distant rumble of traffic to the west. The Drive was a gray-liner, a waterside boulevard running along Lake St. Clair through the older affluent neighborhoods of Grosse Point. That "great point," the first of residential suburbs for the wellborn and wealthy, we admired from our two-wheeler. Our 12 mile per hour pace held steady through Grosse Point Park, then Grosse Point Farms and Grosse Point Shores. Stately homes of the auto magnates and other Wolverine State luminaries beckoned. We could have stopped in "The Farms" to visit the mansion of John Dodge and the Alger House (home of Russell Alger, lumber baron and former governor, then U.S. senator in the 1880s — now a branch of the Detroit Institute of Art) but time had us in its linear grip. We wanted to GET THERE!

By dusk, *Sir Walter* had carried me 69 miles to Roseville. I called daughter Cindy in Port Huron, only 36 miles away, merely a half-hour automobile ride via Interstate 94.

She and Linda Ham, her housemate, suggested whisking down to take me to dinner at the Hanger Cafe in Roseville. How wonderful it was to be with family again after 31 days of touring! I don't recall specifically what we talked about, but our reunion was as warm as one can be.

Cindy's one-person family law practice in Port Huron and Linda's adventures as a social worker shared our conversation's center as much as my trip. I was hungry for news other than which was the best route to the next resting place and what the weather predictions contained. I found it difficult to describe anything in other than general terms. There simply was too much to share at one sitting.

"Hey, Pops, how about we take along what you don't need for tomorrow's ride into Pt. Huron? It might be easier if you run into headwinds," Cindy suggested.

"Nothing doing," I replied. I was startled by my unexpected refusal to lighten my load more than Cindy seemed to be. "I've made it this far with a full pack. I want to carry everything across the bridge to Canada, just as though I was going to continue on. It'll be less than 40 miles. Should be easy."

Of course, there was that one more bridge. A big one, span-

PHOTO OF the Bluewater Bridge over the St. Clair River in Michigan, marked the last bridge crossed by the Author.

ning a river between two countries. What about those expansion joints between Michigan and Canada? Would those dragons' teeth be the most formidable of any I had encountered so far? We would know tomorrow.

CHAPTER THIRTEEN

FISHING IN TIME'S STREAM

If one advances confidently in the direction of his dreams and endeavors to live the life he has imagined, he will meet with success unexpected in common hours.

—Thoreau
Walden

During the reunion dinner in Roseville, Cindy and Linda advised that I take Gratiot Avenue (Route 19) to Port Huron. It began as a double redliner on the map but, to my delight, dwindled into a pink, then a gray line as I cycled north-by-northeast. The morning traffic surrounded me, coming and going. Its commuting hum penetrated into the very marrow of my bones. I knew that as I spun away from Detroit's dismal West Jefferson Avenue, the vehicular flow would diminish, but I became increasingly apprehensive, even as I sped away from the Motor City and its affluent suburbs.

I paid particular attention to my position when traffic lights turned from green to red or vice versa. I didn't move along at a red light, edging up on the far right past vehicles to get a clear shot at crossing a throughfare as far out of the traffic flow to the right as possible. Some motorists resent cyclists who edge up on the right. Of course, any sensible biker doesn't race any four-wheeler across an intersection, but we do have a tendency to slide up and into a favorable position while waiting for the light to change. For one thing, the exhaust fumes aren't quite as heavy around us as engines idle if we're at the front of the traffic line. But this morning I stayed back in the line of cars and trucks, well to the right, not edging up as I usually did. Then I realized why I was so uneasy in traffic. I had traveled more than 1,600 miles without even having to add air to my tires! Now, within sight of my goal, I was developing a galloping paranoia. For the first time in my 32 days on the road, I became slightly paranoid about my personal safety.

Those admonishments from my peers echoed: What about all those crazy drivers? How about the nuts who can hit you and run away so easily? What about the drunks? The teen-agers? Why take the chance? You got no protection. You can't get away.

Those last 36 miles became the longest I had ever experienced. Gradually, as the traffic thinned, I managed to shake off my anxieties by assuring myself that urban Michigan drivers are no better or worse than any other geographical group of motorists. Then, as I approached the Port Huron city limits, my adrenalin began to surge. It was like any other June Friday to all of those hurrying on their appointed rounds, but for me it represented much more. I was about to complete my journey, achieve my goal. Just one more bridge to cross.

I really wanted to drop into the Museum of Arts and History on Gratiot Avenue along that home stretch, so to speak. I wanted to get back to the way the land was, archaeologically speaking, and admire the exhibits featuring the Woodlands Indians, Fort Gratiot and Thomas Edison's boyhood home, but I didn't take the time. I did stop in to my daughter's law office on the way to the St. Clair River bridge to Canada, just to tell her I would be back as soon as I had set foot on Canadian soil and mailed postcards to my biking friends back in Florida. None of them was aware I was taking my upcountry tour. Only my wife, Cindy and I had been in on the attempted mini-odyssey.

I basked briefly in the sunshine of attention from Cindy's office mates that Friday morning, then headed for the final crossing. The Bluewater Bridge over the St. Clair River would have been the longest, highest bridge I would have crossed. "Would have" is the operative phrase here. I did cross it, but not in the way I would have preferred.

As I approached the Customs area — remember, I'd be crossing into a foreign country — I was told that I could not ride my bike across the bridge. There were repairs underway, and the two-lane traffic would be too congested. The bridge manager explained that they did have a pedestrian sidewalk, but that, too, was blocked on the Michigan-to-Canada direction.

Well, why couldn't I just take my chances on the Canada-to-Michigan sidewalk? I'd walk *Sir Walter* across the span, even though it was more than 6,000 feet long. Please. I've come 1,600 miles to cross this bridge. Can't I just do it? The Bluewater Bridge official was very polite, but quite firm.

"Tell you what," he said. "I'll get somebody to take you across in a pickup, then, when you want to come back, we'll send somebody over to tote you back. How's that?"

"Guess it'll have to do," I sighed. And that's how I ended my mini-odyssey. Of course, the manager was right. As we crept across the span in bumper-to-bumper traffic, I realized how important it was to keep the flow going during the bridge repair period. Ironically, I realized as we passed over the huge expansion joints that I could have hopped off *Sir Walter* and carried him across the dragon's teeth in that snail's pace traffic. Ah well, I had cycled all but the final two miles to Canada. So be it.

I didn't spent much time in Sarnia (pop. 68,700), located at the south edge of Lake Huron in the heart of a large industrial-agricultural area. Besides the Bluewater Bridge, there also was a railroad tunnel connecting Port Huron with Sarnia. That port city handles a large volume of freight for trans-shipment from railroads to Great Lakes steamers. I could see towering grain elevators and an oil refinery as I was hauled across the huge span. Chemical and synthetic rubber industries also are located downriver from the Bluewater Bridge.

Sir Walter and I did travel far enough into Sarnia to find a variety store and magazine shop where we got our postcards. Clearing Customs had been effortless. I carried no firearms, and my pannier bags were not searched to see if I was telling the truth. However, that was in 1994. Perhaps, in this increasingly terrorist-threatened age, my gear would have been x-rayed.

Returning to Port Huron aboard another Bridge Authority

pickup truck was uneventful. Retaining our postures as mountain-conquering, upcountry travelers was difficult for *Sir Walter* and me, crouching behind the pickup's cab, but the mild humiliation was soon over and we were released to our own choice of stateside pathways.

As we meandered back to my daughter's law office, I became increasingly cognizant of the comparative ease of travel anywhere in the U.S.A. No border guards between Florida and Georgia, or Kentucky and Ohio. Not even a passport was necessary to cross the Bluewater Bridge to Canada. The thought of a military coup in Virginia that would threaten my safety was laughable. North Carolina would never close its borders to those of any minority race, ethnic group, or religious persuasion. Tennessee border guards refusing visitors from Kentucky, Virginia or North Carolina? Unthinkable.

We take our pluralistic society for granted. One of our most precious of national possessions, our freedom of movement across the borders of individual states and bordering nations, is assumed a birthright. Tell this to any former Yugoslavians who are of Croatian, Bosnian, or Serbian descent. What we have some of them would lay down their lives for. Some have already.

I returned to Cindy's law office for a late afternoon informal celebration of my arrival. More than forty of her business associates and friends dropped in to meet me and wish me well. Fortunately, I didn't have to acknowledge all of the informal accolades with a formal speech. The most memorable bit of conversation I overheard during that happy two hours had nothing to do with my trip. I recall a Port Huron area judge telling my daughter, a relative newcomer to the legal profession, that her trial skills were to be commended. How proud I was to be there with her.

That weekend was memorable for its community warmth and personal family pleasures. Sunday, June 19, was Father's Day. From the pulpit of the Zion Lutheran Church, Pastor Ted Menter remarked, his eyes twinkling toward us as Cindy and I sat together in pews at the rear of the church, "I don't know if I would ride 1,600 miles on a bike to be with my daughter."

Roberta Stevenson, a Port Huron *Herald* feature writer, had interviewed me during the Friday evening office party, and her story appeared during the week I remained in Port Huron before returning to West Palm Beach via Amtrak train. I was told that her upbeat description of my upcountry trip apparently sparked several calls to the newspaper complimenting it on its "positive" approach to that day's news.

As I look back on my excellent adventure I'm reminded of a remark made by NASA astrophysicist Dr. Laurence Doyle regarding man's concept of the passing of time. During a radio interview, he stated, "If people think of time as a limitation in terms of opportunity or health, [they should realize] there is no relationship of the orbit of the planet around the sun and the aging of the human body. Time is merely the relative motion of matter being redundant."

As I write this narrative, I'm entering my 70s. Far too many folks my age think their lives have lost some of their luster because all of us have been led to believe aging is inevitable, that we can't try new things because we're "too old." Dr. Doyle's remarks about time deny this attitude. There IS no connection between our individual ages and the turning of the clock's hands. Certainly, some of us are older than others, but it's not because of our chronological age. Parts of us simply age at different rates, and 99 percent of our cells can repair themselves. I believe they have individual memories, and the stress of worry, fear, anxiety impairs their ability to renew themselves.

All of this continuing scientific research reminds us that we must cast aside the idea that our passing birthdays place limits on what we want to do with our lives as time passes. We humans, as the ages pass, are developing ever more sophisticated ways of keeping track of time for an ever-increasing variety of reasons, scientific and otherwise. But we must not let ourselves become victims of our own inventions.

In Thoreau's *Walden*, he writes, "Time is a stream I go fishing in..." That is, we all are existing together in the past, present

ROAD SIGN reminded me to not only call home most nights, but also to "Never put life on hold."

and future at the same time. We can dip into this vast dimension in search of whatever we choose. We can fish for anything we desire by using as bait our imaginations and our wills to set goals for ourselves and stride toward them. How lucky we are with our "catches" depends upon our skills as "fishermen."

Deepak Chopra, in his *Ageless Body, Timeless Mind*, explains in scientific terms what Thoreau alludes to with his fishing in the stream-of-time metaphor: "No matter how separate anything appears to the senses, nothing is separate at the quantum level. The quantum field exists in, around and through you. You are not looking at the field — in every wave and particle, the field is your extended body."

It is not my intention to pretend an intimate knowledge of quantum physics, but only to urge every reader of this upcountry narrative to look beyond the ticking clock to the endless horizons of our boundless imaginations. Spread those wonderful maps of our known worlds before you, whether they be the familiar *DeLorme* or *Rand McNally* wonders of detailed geographic paths available to us or words in books or pictures on screens. Begin your trips among those beckoning fields. It is never too late.

APPENDIX A —
NAVIGATIONAL SOURCES

DeLorme Mapping Atlases and Gazetteers ("Back Road Maps" and "Topo Maps") of individual states. For information: DeLorme Mapping, P.O. Box 298, Freeport, ME 04032 or phone (207)865-4171.

Rand McNally Road Atlases — Rand McNally & Company, P.O. Box 564, Skokie, IL 60076

County maps — Write to the Departments of Transportation of the individual states. They are located in the capitals. Some charge nominal fees for maps. These provide the most up-to-date information about paved roads in rural areas.

Adventure Cycling, Inc — Very detailed maps, primarily of routes most frequently requested by cyclists. Strong on maps of west and northwest, plus coast-to-coast treks. Only two of available maps were useful in my route, those in western Virginia that were primarily designed for west-to-east travel.

Cyclists interested in riding around Lake Okeechobee might take the BIG-0-Bike Tour, sponsored by the Greater Lake Okeechobee Tourism Alliance, 1-800-871-4403. The third annual tour (1997) was expected to draw more than 100 riders. Three days, 110 miles, camping three nights. Bring own gear. Not for beginners. Fat tire and touring bikes only. Tires should be at least 700x35 (metric) or a similar width on an older rim. Easiest size wheel for the top of the dike would be 27 inches, in my opinion. Check with your local bike shop. All rim and tire sizes these days are in metric sizes. Old *Sir Walter* has 27-inch wheels. The tires I used were 700 x 35s.

APPENDIX B —
EQUIPMENT AND TRAVEL EXPENSES

Long-distance bicycle touring in the United States began on April 22,1884 when Thomas Stevens, an Englishman, left San Francisco for New York City. It took him 103½ days on a Columbia High Wheeler with hard rubber tires! He passed covered wagons coming west along the Platt River, followed railroad tracks and canal tow paths. It's hard to imagine the hardships involved traveling over the roads, paths and trails of that time, because there weren't any paved roads to speak of. Today, there are unlimited paved roads to travel. Since 1976, the year of the U.S. Bicentennial, more than 10,000 folks have ridden coast-to-coast on bicycles.

What's the best bike to use? It's up to you. You can spend from about $600 to more than $2,000 on a touring bike. My bike was a gift, a 20-year-old Raleigh Super Course. It was a road bike, but not really a long-distance touring bike. That is, the wheel base (distance between the front wheel axle and the rear axle) was shorter than a touring bike's wheel base. It makes for bumpier riding, but one endures. Real luxury is riding the tandem Kate and I enjoy together. Because of its longer wheel base, it rides much more smoothly.

You'll want to use fatter tires than old *Sir Walter* was equipped with when he was much younger. I "shod" him with 700 x 35s. They're wider than what he had before. I replaced his original 27-inch (diameter) wheels with new ones. The 700 x 35s fit those wheels. The bike weighed 40 pounds, unloaded. This included a rear rack (Blackburn).

An estimated 80% of the bicycles sold today are mountain bikes. They are designed for on and offroad riding, but not really for touring long distances.

Long-distance, self-contained touring also requires frames and panniers (reinforced saddlebags) on both front and back wheels. My front panniers cost $40.00. The rear one cost $39.00. Front panniers (one on each side of the wheel) cost

$80.00 for the pair. A pair of back panniers cost $90.

The smallest, lightest two-person tent I could find, including a rain fly, was $120. There are smaller tents, but the extra room for another person was used to protect my gear from rain and nighttime dampness.

My air mattress was $55, and an ultra lightweight sleeping bag was $100. My single-burner stove (Whisper) was $62.50. It could boil water for coffee in one minute.

Food, mostly prepared by somebody else, totaled $488.08 for the 32 days I was on the road, an average of about $15 per day.

Lodging totaled $499.35, averaging about $27 a day. The cheapest (black-and-white TV) motel was $18 (rural South Carolina). The most expensive was $38 (Blowing Rock, North Carolina).

My costs for touring equipment, meals, lodging and incidentals totalled slightly more than $1,700 for the 32 days on the road.